How to Take Tests

How to Take Tests

by Sara Gilbert

William Morrow and Company
New York   1983

ACKNOWLEDGEMENTS: In writing *How to Take Tests,* the author has relied greatly upon the contributions of many expert organizations and individuals.

She would like to thank especially the counselors, advisors, and the testing and tutoring specialists at Anne Arundel Community College in Arnold, Maryland, for their generosity in sharing ideas and materials.

The following educational and testing organizations provided abundant supplies of their guides and samples: Addison-Wesley Testing Service; American College Testing Program; American School Counselors Association; College Entrance Examination Board; CTB/McGraw Hill; Educational Records Bureau; Educational Testing Service; Harcourt Brace Jovanovich; National Association of Secondary School Principals; National Education Association; National Institute of Education; The Psychological Corporation; Science Research Associates; University of the State of New York, State Education Department.

Copyright © 1983 by Sara D. Gilbert

All rights reserved. No part of this book may be reproduced or utilized in any form or by any means, electronic or mechanical, including photocopying, recording or by any information storage and retrieval system, without permission in writing from the Publisher. Inquiries should be addressed to William Morrow and Company, Inc.
105 Madison Avenue
New York, N.Y. 10016.

Printed in the United States of America.
10 9 8 7 6 5 4 3 2

Library of Congress Cataloging in Publication Data
Gilbert, Sara D. How to take tests.
Includes bibliographies and index. Summary: Discusses the most effective ways to study and to take tests, including quizzes, final exams, and standardized tests, successfully, emphasizing the method of preview, view, and review.

1. Examinations—Study guides—Juvenile literature. 2. Educational tests and measurements—Study guides—Juvenile literature. [1. Examinations—Study guides. 2. Study, Method of] I. Title.
LB3051.G514   1983   371.26   83-7115
ISBN 0-688-02469-6
ISBN 0-688-02470-X (pbk.)

*This book is for my son, Sean,
who knows how to take tests of all sorts.*

Contents

Facts of Life	1

Section One: Before the Tests

1. Preview: 4
WHAT THIS BOOK WILL DO FOR YOU
Preview, View, Review ... It's Not Fair! ... Become Testwise ... How to Face the Facts of Life ...

2. How to Take a Test: 13
THE BASIC STEPS
Preview ... View ... Review ...

3. Toward Better Study Skills: 29
PREVIEW, VIEW, REVIEW
Get to Know Yourself ... Attitude Counts ... Getting the Most Out of Your Classwork ... Read It Right ... Cramming ... All Work and No Play ...

4. Nothing to Be Afraid Of: 42
PSYCHING UP AND COOLING DOWN
Looking Back ... Psyching Up ... Cooling Down ...

Section Two: The Tests

5. The "Small Stuff":   54
Quizzes and Tests—and the Forms They Take
Why Bother? ... What's in It for You? ... Asking the Right Questions ... The Forms Tests Take ... Where Grades Come From ...

6. Bigger Deals: 80
Course Exams and How to Prepare for Each Type
How to Cope ... Buckle Down ... Make Your Memory Work ... Take a Deep Breath! ... Just in Case ... Meeting the Test ...

7. Taking the Mystery Out of Standardized Tests: 95
What They Are and Why
Why Were Those Tests Ever Invented? ... What You're Up Against: Different Types of Standardized Tests ... What These Tests Are Testing ... How You Get What You Get ...

8. Preparing for Standardized Tests: 106
You *Can* Coach Yourself
Where to Start ... Testing Formats ... Technicalities ... In the Testing Room ... Dealing with Directions ... Taking the Test ... What to Expect ...

Section Three: Beyond the Tests

9. **Follow Through:**   126
   MAKING THE MOST OF YOUR EFFORTS
   Unraveling Those Mysterious Numbers ... Student Rights ... Using Your Grades as a Guide ...

10. **Making a Good Impression:**   130
    OTHER FACTORS IN SCHOOL SUCCESS
    Watch Your Image ... A Quick Word About Cheating ...

11. **Review!**   135

Practice, Practice, Practice

Commonly Administered Standardized Tests   138

Sources for Further Information   152
Books and Study Guides ... Test-Taking Workbooks ... Language Skills Study Guides ... Test Publishers ... Organizations ... Coaching and Tutoring Schools ...

Index   161

Facts of Life

Tests are a fact of life, and you are at a stage when they are one of the most important facts of life that you have to face.

Since you have opened this book, you probably

1. understand how important tests are in your life, or
2. feel a bit nervous about taking tests, or
3. both of the above

Tests *are* important. Even little quizzes can have a big effect on you, so you are right to seek out all the help you can, including paying attention to the experts' advice that you'll find in this book.

A few schools include study skills and test-taking techniques as part of their programs; but too often, students are simply told that they will "Have an exam next week"—and that serves only to scare. "What do I do about that?" "How can I stuff that information into my head?" "What will happen to me if I don't get a good grade?"

Tests *do* scare many people. But the more you know about them—what they are, why they are, and how to deal with them—the less scary they are. That's what this book is about: the what, why, and how of every kind of test.

Section One: Before the Tests

1. Preview:

WHAT THIS BOOK WILL DO FOR YOU

As a student, I was a successful test taker; often I got better scores and grades than my grasp of the information deserved. But like most "testwise" people, I wasn't really aware of using any special system. Now, having read and talked with educators and experts in the field of educational psychology, I've learned that I was studying and taking tests in the "recommended" way.

The naturally testwise among your classmates don't have to be the only ones who do well on exams, because it is really not so hard to learn how to take a test.

PREVIEW, VIEW, REVIEW

The most effective way to study, and to take tests successfully, say the experts, is to preview, view, review: to look over all the material first; then to work at it; and finally to go back through it all again when you are finished.

This is the pattern you will see repeated throughout the book.

In this section you will find out what you need to know and do before you take a test. Section II will help you tackle the kinds of tests you are likely to *view* both now and later, including all the major standardized tests. Section III reviews the key points for effective studying and successful test taking, and discusses what you can do after and in addition to test taking to get the most from your efforts.

This book will probably *not* help you enjoy tests or look forward to them. Nor can it guarantee that every test you take will be an "easy A." But the studying and test-taking techniques that you learn here will help you to approach tests in ways that will probably improve your grades.

IT'S NOT FAIR!

The first step in this approach is to accept the fact that you do have to take tests, both in school and out—so there's not much point in wasting energy on protesting the reality of tests.

Like you, many people feel that tests are not fair. Students have always griped, sometimes with reason, about tests, and wished that they never had to face them. Educators and other experts also question their fairness. A few believe that tests do not have a place in education. Many more criticize the tests that are in use, both in individual classrooms and nationally, for being unfairly designed or graded.

Regardless, the fact is that, fair or not, tests exist and they are important. Even a quiz may give your teacher an impression of you—good or bad—that can be hard to alter. More important classroom tests and exams affect or determine your grades for a course. By your grades, of course, you pass or fail. In that very real way they set the direction for your life. Like the minimum competency tests many school systems require, they determine the next steps that you can take after you leave school.

Equally important, those grades go into your permanent record, and that permanent record makes up a portrait of you—the most significant one that an employer or an advanced-education admissions officer will ever see.

Standardized aptitude and achievement tests add even more detail to that portrait. Rightly or wrongly, they tell important people in your present and future what you can or can't be, should or shouldn't do: who you are or who you will be.

All of these hard facts might make you angry, because it is not really fair that a few pieces of paper can have such an influence on your life. What can you do about them? You can learn to take tests successfully. You can become testwise.

BECOME TESTWISE

The testwise members of your class are not necessarily the brightest ones. They may not even be the hardest workers. But they know how to study and prepare. They also have a positive attitude, and a relaxed approach that comes from knowing how to take tests. They don't have to waste time or energy sweating over the specific techniques demanded by each type of test question. For instance . . .

A. When they read a question like this, they know exactly what is being asked:

Preview

Define the difference between this test-taking guide and others, comparing and contrasting the contents of the two types by describing both. Evaluate both types, supporting your argument with a detailed example chosen from each. Summarize your response in outline form.

B. When they face a page from any of these standardized tests:

>   SAT
>   ACT
>   ITED
>   SRA
>   SSAT
>   NEDT

they know on which it's better to guess at possible right answers, and on which they should skip the items they're unsure of.

C. When they see a series of questions like this, they know which ones to answer first:

	True	False
1. All students find exams difficult.	____	____
2. A quiz is less likely to be important for a student's grade than a midterm exam.	____	____
3. Clues to the answer are never given in the question.	____	____
4. Test takers can expect true-false answers to follow a pattern, such as T F F T F.	____	____

5. The true-false part of a test is always counted as the least important. _____ _____

D. They would know the first thing to do if confronted with a test like this:

   1. Define the area of this triangle:

   2. If a = 6, then 24b = __?__

   3. Find x: 37 = 42 5

   4. 82
      <u> 7</u>

   5. If a swimmer is rowing upstream at 5 miles per hour, how fast is the river flowing downstream?

E. And they know the last step to take whenever they work a test like this:

   1. Multiple-choice tests are ____ common type of exam.
      a. many
      b. simple
      c. one
      d. NONE OF THE ABOVE

   2. You must be ____ when answering a multiple-choice question.
      a. careful
      b. relaxed
      c. right
      d. ALL OF THE ABOVE

Preview

3. Multiple-choice questions are _____ scored with the same weight as other types of questions.
   a. never
   b. always
   c. sometimes
   d. ALL OF THE ABOVE

4. When working a multiple-choice question, you should _____ the possible answers first.
   a. read
   b. mark
   c. ignore
   d. NONE OF THE ABOVE

5. A multiple-choice test is not the _____ type of exam that requires reviewing.
   a. best
   b. only
   c. LEAVE BLANK
   d. NONE OF THE ABOVE

Would you approach these tests the way that testwise students do? If so, in Part A, you would know the exact meanings of the key words in the instructions: "define," "comparing," "contrasting," "describing," "evaluate," "supporting," "summarize," and "outline." (If you don't, pages 71-77 list the definitions of these and other important instruction phrases.)

Part B lists common standardized achievement tests. Of this list, only the SAT (the Scholastic Aptitude Test) subtracts points from your total score for every wrong answer. Chapter 8 will give further details about guessing or not guessing on standardized tests.

Which questions to answer first? Always start with the easiest. In true-false questions like those in Part C, statements that contain absolute words like "all," "never," or "always" are almost always false, so questions 1, 3, and 5 count as the easiest here.

Did you notice that the items in Part D are each missing some vital information? You would have no way to solve these problems without some more symbols and numbers. So the first step to take in a situation like this is to ask for the needed details.

Part E could be any type of test, because the last step that every successful tester takes on *any* exam is to review the test and recheck the answers. (This is especially important on multiple-choice questions, since it is so simple to mark the wrong item.)

As you can see, none of these techniques has anything to do with the knowledge that exams are supposed to test—yet each of them is vital to scoring well.

HOW TO FACE THE FACTS OF LIFE

Successful test taking is not just a matter of how much you know. It is a skill in itself, and one that you can learn and practice in the next chapters.

You will find this skill useful, no matter what your grade or level of education. It is a surprising fact that most "how-to-study" books and programs are designed for college students. If you're in college now and haven't yet learned how to take a test, it's certainly time! If you're in junior high school, your test grades are just beginning to play important roles in your life and future. The study and exam-taking skills you learn here will last you through high school and beyond, for they are like bicycle riding: once learned, never forgotten. And that's lucky, because many people who thought that their test-taking days ended with their schooling find that they must score well on one sort of exam or another to get jobs or gain promotions throughout their lives.

Does the very thought of that make you nervous? Don't worry—You'll find techniques in Chapter 4 that will help you overcome the tension that rises in many people when they must take a test of any kind.

When you have learned the study skills, test-taking techniques, and relaxation systems described in this book, you will probably find that you get better grades on your tests, since the methods described have been proven to increase learning and retention ability and efficiency. You will certainly feel better about taking tests—and confidence is a vital key to high scoring in any competition.

Because familiarity with the material is the best guarantee of doing well on any test, go through the various question-form examples—short answer, multiple choice, problem solving, and essay—in Chapter 5. And since warmup is as important to test taking as it is to exercise or sports, begin with quizzes and other exams that most people don't consider too much of a worry and work your way up toward the standardized tests that turn so many students into zombies. Start with the so-called small stuff in Chapter 5, because the tips you learn there are equally valuable for—and apply just as much to—the "big deals" of Chapter 6 and the standardized tests of Chapter 8.

You'll find that "working your way up" is the best way to study, in any case. Our minds are much more capable of grasping and retaining information that is taken in small doses over a period of time than of handling material that's crammed into them at the last minute. Still, if you must cram, you'll find help here on how to do that, too.

Whether you're cramming, studying methodically for an exam, taking a standardized test, or simply reading an assignment in advance of a class discussion, you will learn how to go about it. You'll learn to

preview: to survey and skim the material first
view: to go through the body of the material with care
review: to give everything a final once-over, to lock in what you've read or to check the accuracy of what you've written

For practice, and to prepare your mind to take in the most of what this book has to offer, flip through the following chapters and preview the techniques that you will be learning before you begin reading in earnest.

2. How to Take a Test:

THE BASIC STEPS

Few people would follow the advice given at the end of the last chapter. Most would have simply gone on reading. Yet flipping through the whole book first for a preview before reading again more slowly and carefully is the best way to approach this or any other learning material.

Preview, view, review—this is the pattern to follow when studying for and taking a test. Testwise students follow this approach, and once you get into the habit, you'll find that you, too, will probably remember more, so that no quiz or test will be impossible.

Experts in the psychology of learning recommend such a step-by-step procedure because it effectively triggers the memory and sets in motion something called *latent learning*. Though you may not be consciously aware of it, the preview stage activates the back of your mind, so that by the time you are ready to actually answer (or view) the questions, the responses have begun to move to the front of your consciousness. When you save time for the review stage, you will find that questions that seemed impossible at first are a lot easier, because your brain has been stimulated to work at them.

This pattern proves efficient in practical terms, too. It helps you to know ahead of time what you need to do, allows you to do it, and permits time afterward to make sure you did what you intended.

PREVIEW

Too often, when students face a test paper, they feel such pressure from the time limit or from their shaky grasp of the required information that they immediately plunge into the first problem or question without reading through the directions or giving any thought for the overall test. Testwise students, however, know that the investment of a certain amount of effort and time in previewing it—about one-tenth the total time allowed for the test—can bring most worthwhile rewards. So:

- Before you start working on the test, read or listen to the instructions carefully:

Did the teacher say to write on *every other* line?

Are you supposed to put your name in the right-hand or the left-hand corner? Last, or first, name first?

Should you underline, circle, or X out the right answer in a multiple choice? Or the wrong answers?

Is there a time limit?

Will extra points be lost for errors, or is it safe to guess at answers?

How to Take a Test

Do you use pen or pencil?

If the teacher is reading the test questions, are you supposed to write down the questions as well as the answers, or only the answers?

Can you work on the entire test in whatever order you choose, or must you go section by section?

Often students are so eager to begin—or to get it over with—that they don't pay proper attention to the instructions for the exam. Or they may find a teacher's instructions irritating or silly, so simply ignore them. Most classroom teachers have reasons for requiring precision in following instructions: Either they have designed the quiz or test to be graded according to a specific pattern; or they are trying to help their students learn to follow instructions to the letter in preparation for the standardized tests that are scored electronically and give no leeway for misfollowed instructions. No matter what the test, remember that the instructions are a *part* of it.

Follow all directions *exactly*. You might answer an entire section wrong if you have not read the instructions properly. You can lose out completely if your answers are not in the right form.

To be sure that you take this advice seriously, think about the following examples:

WORK THIS TEST IN 20 MINUTES

  I. If any of the following statements is false, circle *T* after it.

     1. Only smart students do well on tests.   T F

2. A course in study skills is an important part of all school programs. T F
3. Tests never scare people. T F
4. This book guarantees you an A on every test. T F
5. Nobody feels that tests are fair. T F

II. Answer these problems in decimal form.

1. ½ + ¼ = _____

2. 3/4 − 2/8 = _____

3. ¼ × ¼ = _____

4. 5/10 ÷ 3/12 = _____

5. What is the next number in this sequence: 1/10, 2/10, 3/10, 4/10, _____

III. Complete each of the following sentences with a word beginning with the letter *s*.

1. Some of the people who object to testing procedures are _____.

2. Those who know how to take tests often find them _____.

3. Among the tests that can have the biggest influence on your life are those that we call _____.

4. Since you are reading this book, you probably take tests _____.

How to Take a Test

5. Students who have scored significantly higher on previous exams find that when they face a new one, they feel _____.

IV. In the following statements, underline each noun that is a subject, circle each subject that is not plural, **X** out each noun that is not a subject, and put a dot beside every subject that is not a noun.

    1. They always give tests when students least expect them. _____

    2. A teacher may sometimes give a test as a punishment. _____

    3. Many students are afraid of tests because they do not feel good about themselves. _____

    4. The quick brown fox jumped over the lazy sleeping dog. _____

    5. The only thing we have to fear is fear itself. _____

V. Arrange the answers to these problems in numerical order, biggest to smallest.

    1. $5 + 6 =$ _____   _____

    2. $12 - 7 =$ _____   _____

    3. $4 + 2 =$ _____   _____

    4. $12 \div 3 =$ _____   _____

    5. $1 \times 7 =$ _____   _____

VI. In these "fill-in-the-blank" sentences, do not fill in the blanks.

1. You are probably reading this book because you are _____ about taking tests.

2. Students who know how to take tests are called _____.

3. The best pattern to follow for studying and test-taking is preview, _____, review.

4. Section II of this book details hints about taking each type of _____.

5. If you have filled in the blanks in the above questions, you are in _____.

VII. With a pencil, connect the words in Column A with those in Column B that have the same number of letters.

A	B
test	fret
exam	aid
grade	paper
score	numbered
practice	order
study	previews
try	scale
worry	guess
help	trial

VIII. In the following sentences, circle the words that do not contain an *e*.

1. Define what is meant by being testwise in terms of the intelligence of the test taker, the ability to read instructions, and the approach to the test itself.

How to Take a Test

2. Outline the best procedure for studying and for taking tests.

3. Compare and contrast the difference between the way you take tests and the way the testwise student does.

4. Explain why you are reading this book.

5. The instructions told you only to circle the words that did not contain an *e*. If you followed those instructions, why? If not, why not?

IX. Define the following words that have fewer than four letters.
   1. test _____
   2. grade _____
   3. review _____
   4. guess _____

5. try _____
6. numbered _____
7. standardized _____
8. scale _____

X. To this list of words relating to testing, add six on another topic.

exam _____ _____

study _____ _____

score _____ _____

XI. The following paragraph contains a number of errors. Ignore the errors and circle any word that applies to test taking.

Tests (1) <u>is</u> a way of evaluating students. (2) <u>Being as they</u> are a means of measuring a (3) <u>students'</u> potential, (4) <u>you</u> ought to be (5) <u>admiring</u> various elements (6) <u>regarding as how</u> tests can be (7) <u>of beneficial</u> to anyone as a test taker. Testwise students know how to approach (8) <u>exams, being used</u> to the process. Once you have learned how to take examinations, it will be easier for you to (9) <u>do good</u> on tests. (10) <u>Consequence</u> shows that ability to pass examinations (11) <u>will be greatly enhanced</u>.

1. _____   7. _____
2. _____   8. _____
3. _____   9. _____
4. _____   10. _____
5. _____   11. _____
6. _____

How to Take a Test

XII. Read all these questions before answering any of them. *Answer* by circling the correct letter, or letters.

1. The best way to take a test is to
   - (a) study.
   - (b) preview first.
   - (c) be careful.
   - (d) don't panic.
   - (e) all of the above.

2. Test taking is
   - (a) hard.
   - (b) a skill in itself.
   - (c) easy when you know how.
   - (d) something that takes practice.
   - (e) all of the above.

3. You can do poorly on a test if
   - (a) you haven't studied.
   - (b) you are scared.
   - (c) you've done poorly before.
   - (d) you don't know the answers.
   - (e) all of the above.

4. This book will
   - (a) not give you all the answers.
   - (b) help develop your study skills.
   - (c) help you feel better about tests.
   - (d) share secrets of testwise students.
   - (e) all of the above.

5. Do not answer any of the above questions. Answer only this item. You have now learned that
   - (a) you don't follow instructions as well as you thought you did.
   - (b) you do follow instructions well.

(c) sometimes all the answers on a multiple-choice test are "correct."
(d) instructions are a crucial part of any test.
(e) none of the above.

The following are *not* the answers to the preceding quizzes! Rather, they are analyses of the *instructions* to those quizzes.

I. The instruction was to circle *T* for every *false* answer. Did you do that?

II. The instructions asked for answers in decimal form. What form did you use?

III. The test taker was directed to use only words beginning with *s*. How many did you think of?

IV. Did you *answer* each statement by filling in the blank? Or did you *follow* each direction? Read the instructions again, word for word, to see how you did.

V. What numerical order did you put your answers in?

VI. Anyone who filled in the blanks failed this test.

VII. Did you match all the *same-length* words?

VIII. Did you answer each question—or instead circle all the *e*-less words, as the instructions asked?

IX. How many words did you define? According to the directions, "try" is the only word you should have.

X. You could have added any six words, as long as they had nothing to do with tests or grades.

XI. What did you do here—correct the grammar, or circle all test-related words?

XII. If you answered any question before 5, your answer to the last question is 5a, c, and d. If you did *not* answer any question before 5, your answer is 5b, c, and d—and
Congratulations!

Testwise students would have done perfectly on all of those perhaps silly examples, because they would have read the directions accurately. It is *that* important to read and understand the instructions provided with any tests.

If you do not understand any or all of them—*ask!* There are some tests on which it is to your advantage to guess at the answers. It is *never* to your advantage to guess at instructions. The worst that can happen when you raise your hand for a clarification is that the teacher or test monitor will say, "You have to figure that out for yourself"—in which case, you are no worse off. The best that can happen is that you will receive help that will enable you to work the test properly—in which case, you are much better off.

If the test is an oral one, in which the teacher dictates the questions, you need to pay even closer attention. Jot down a few key words of each question so that you can remember them should you have to go back. If you need to, ask the teacher to repeat the question. And again, if you are confused, ask, no matter how silly you may feel. You will feel even sillier if you mess up because you didn't understand something.

- Read through the entire test (or as much of it as you are allowed to see at one time) quickly. As you skim, make a note, either mentally or jotted on scrap paper, about which questions or sections

> seem easiest or hardest
> count for the most and the least
> you don't, at first glance, understand completely.

By doing that, even for a short quiz, you will

1. gain an important overall picture of what the test is about, and
2. start the back of your mind working in advance on the more puzzling items.

For instance, if you are instructed to correct the grammar and usage for the following paragraph, by skimming through it you will get an immediate feel for the changes you know must be made. By the time you start making those corrections, you will be much better able to select the right word for Item 5 or the correct punctuation for Item 8.

> Tests (1) is a way of evaluating students. (2) Being as they are a means of measuring a (3) students' potential, (4) you ought to be (5) admiring various elements (6) regarding as how tests can be (7) of beneficial to anyone as a test taker. Testwise students know how to approach (8) exams, being used to the process. Once you have learned how to take examinations, it will be easier for you to (9) do good on tests. (10) Consequence shows that ability to pass examinations (11) will be greatly enhanced.

Or you can start your unconscious mind working on the

essay section of a test while you're figuring the easy true-false questions.

- Plan out how much of your allotted time to spend on each question or problem. Many very bright and well-prepared test takers do poorly on quizzes and exams because they pour too much of themselves into one question that either interests or baffles them, so that they have too little time to work on the rest. Planning, even for a few seconds, is a vital part of the preview stage of test taking.

When you are allotting time, one factor to consider is the weight that each question or section will carry in your test score. If the instructions do not include that information, *ask*. Otherwise, you might end up spending half of the test time on an item that counts toward one-twentieth of your grade!

However, allow more time for essays than for short-answer and multiple-choice questions, because essays take longer. For example, if you have an hour to work the test questions in Chapter 1, you should allow at least twenty minutes (or one-third the time) for the essay, even though it's one-fifth of the test. You should also leave the essay for last, since you can always finish it in outline form if time gets short.

- Take a deep breath! The ability to relax is important to any form of competition, in test taking as well as in athletics, and relaxation before an exam can be as easy as taking a deep breath. Try this now: Close your eyes, then take a deep breath and hold it for a count of ten. Slowly release the breath, and open your eyes. *Or:* Clench every muscle in your body and hold your breath. Maintain that tightness for a count of ten, and then gradually relax and start breathing. If you've done either or both of those simple exercises correctly, you will feel a lessening of tension in your body. Chapter 4 will detail more extensive relaxation procedures, but those two are important first steps when facing an exam of any sort.

VIEW

Now, and only now, are you ready to actually take the test. Many students might think that a preview wastes valuable time, but this preparation is worthwhile. Your understanding of the instructions and your overview of the questions will enable you to cope effectively with the exam as a whole. Here's the way that experts recommend you proceed.

- Answer the easiest questions or work the easiest problems *first*. This ensures that you will get at least part of the test right, and it gives the back of your mind time to chew over the hard ones a bit.
- Go back to the tougher items. Reread them, and think about them from as many angles as possible, trying to relate them to something similar you've done in class or for homework.

Brainstorm rather than think, "I can't do it"—open your head and let all your ideas flood out.

Look for clues within the question itself. For example, in Test E on page 8, you will find that the "clue" in Question 1 lies partly in grammar: Answer (c)—"one"—is the only word of those given that fits grammatically into the sentence.

- If you have any questions about the items on your quiz, exam, or test, and you haven't yet asked them, do it now. You would have a terrible time doing Test D on page 8 if

How to Take a Test

you didn't ask for clarification, since *all* of those problems mean nothing without proper explanation.

- Remember your time allotments, and don't wrestle too long with any one item. If you've looked for clues, if you've racked your brain, if you've tried to get help from the test giver and still can't come up with an answer that seems comfortably right, write it off.

But if the form of the test allows it, try to put *something* down on the paper to show that you did make an effort: part of the calculations for a math problem; a few dates for a history question; some of your thoughts about why an item might be either true or false; the outline for an essay. You may at least get some credit for showing that you tried.

REVIEW

Like previewing, reviewing is an important stage that many students must force themselves to learn. No matter how confident—or shaky—you feel about your answers on a quiz or test, you can never lose, and you can often gain, by going over your paper.

Before you turn it in, check to make sure that you have put down what you had intended. Are your answers clearly marked or written? If your "7" looks like a "9," you won't get credit. Have you circled both "A" and "B"? That answer is no good. If you've marked the wrong answer line throughout a standardized test, you will come up with a negative score.

Is your writing readable? If the test giver can't read your answer on an essay question or a "fill-in-the-blank," you won't get credit.

Unless the instructions say otherwise, it's a good idea to use all the time allowed: there's always room for improvement (and sitting through a test makes a good impression on teachers).

Preview, view, review. As you read through this book, you will learn how useful that general pattern is for taking specific types of tests—from classroom quizzes through standardized tests. The same pattern applies to another step in preparing for exams: studying for them.

3. Toward Better Study Skills:

PREVIEW, VIEW, REVIEW

Some people do well on exams without ever seeming to study; others study all the time without doing so well. Why? The answer has less to do with relative "intelligence" than with the ability to study in the right way.

You will do better on tests if you know *how* to study.

That may sound like a very obvious statement, but you might be surprised at how few students know how to study effectively. In fact, it's a good bet that, no matter how well you think you do, you will have picked up at least a few new tips by the time you finish this chapter.

Although the ability to study is vital to learning and to doing well in school, and although psychologists and educational experts know a great deal about how people learn, study skills are rarely taught in schools at any level. Teachers hand out homework assignments and tell you what to learn for a test, but have many of them trained you in *how* best to accomplish these tasks?

On the other hand, they may have been teaching you those skills all along, but you may not have paid attention because of having a fixed, false idea in your mind about what "study" is.

A better word than "study" is "review." When you study material, you want to preview it and then view it again and again from many angles and in the ways that best fit your study style. (You may never have known it, but you *do* have your own "study style"!)

GET TO KNOW YOURSELF

We all have our own strengths and weaknesses, especially, perhaps, when it comes to school. Some students take to languages naturally but don't even try to make an effort at math, because they "can't do it." You may feel that you are terrible at science and math, though English and history are a snap. A negative attitude can easily defeat you, so it's important to get a handle on it.

Why do you feel good at some subjects and rotten at others? Did you have a math teacher once who didn't like you or didn't teach in a way that you understood? Or did you always like science in elementary school because of the teacher or the class? Maybe one or both of your parents is in the habit of saying "I was always great in . . ." and you imagine that you have to follow along. If you're going to do well in the subjects you "can't do," you may have to wipe the slate clean and start out fresh with a better frame of mind.

You might find it useful to learn whether your judgment of your abilities is correct. Talk with your guidance counselor or have your parents do it to find out what your test scores say about your skills. You may well be stronger in some areas than in others, and if so, you can get help from a teacher, tutor, or possibly even a classmate for your weak points. That's a lot better than simply expecting to fail, because when you expect to fail, you are likely to do so.

Now take a close look at your personal study habits.

Are you a procrastinator? Do you always find it easy to put off until tomorrow anything you don't feel like doing today? Then you will need to get tough with yourself about sticking to your study schedule. Always do your homework before doing anything else, and then reward yourself somehow for being good.

Do you know that you "ought" to do well, but you aren't quite sure why? Maybe you need to think about goals. What kind of career are you interested in, or where do you want to go next with your education? If you keep that goal in mind, working hard will be easier. Or you might make a bet with a friend or family member about what grades you'll get for the semester, so your goal would be to win the bet.

Are you the kind of person who's used to having things come fast and easily? That might make you give up too soon when the work is more difficult, so do the hard stuff first.

Are you more interested in getting a task done quickly, no matter what the quality? Then practice telling yourself that the work isn't done until you've gone back and checked it at least once.

Are you a perfectionist, who may be overly critical of the quality of your work? If so, you may try to do much more than is necessary and thus spread your efforts too thin. Or you may take so long to "get it just right" that you never get an assignment done. Try to set time limits within which you must finish your work, no matter what.

Finally, what kind of learner are you? We all have our own learning styles, too. Some people learn well through their ears, some through their eyes, and some through their hands or entire bodies. To get an idea of your own style, ask yourself this: If you wanted to learn the words to a new hit song, could you do it simply by listening to the lyrics a few times on the radio? Would you write down the words as you heard them and then memorize them from the paper? Or would you have to play it on an instrument, or sing along a lot to get the words down?

Could you learn a new swimming stroke just by listening to someone describe it? Could you watch a swimmer doing it and then do it yourself? Or would you need to get into the pool and actually practice before you could get it right?

Think about your answers, because they will indicate what study techniques are best for you. If you learn by hearing, for instance, you may find it especially useful to read your notes or text aloud when you're studying—or even use a tape recorder. If you're a *sight* learner, you'll want to take complete notes and spend a lot of time reading and studying the charts and illustrations in your books. If you learn physically, you'll do well to "push" your notes around by making charts and diagrams, doing all the practice sections in your text, and maybe even acting out your material.

If you understand your personal style, you see why you're having more trouble in some classes than in others, because teachers have their own styles, too. If you're a *visual* learner with a *verbal* teacher, you'll learn the material better if you work at making visual interpretations of the teacher's words. You'll need to *re*view according to your own style.

ATTITUDE COUNTS

To study effectively, you have to *want* to do well. The words "study" and "student" come from an old Latin word meaning "eager." You may be eager, at least in some of your courses, to learn just for the sake of absorbing knowledge. You may be eager for good grades and test scores at this level of your education so that you have a chance to choose from among the best schools when you reach the next level.

Whatever your personal motivation for success, you do need to have a positive attitude. You might not feel exactly eager, but you should want to learn and use good study and test-taking habits. The fact that you are reading this book is a sign of your positive attitude.

Students who have this attitude show it by attending class regularly, by paying attention, and by taking notes. They do homework assignments carefully and on time, and when they miss a class or an assignment, they take responsibility for making up what they missed.

Such conscientious behavior is beneficial in two ways. It guarantees that when exam time comes, you will have all the material you need for study and review. It also makes a good impression on the teacher—and this is an important part of success.

So think for a moment about *your* attitude. Why do you want to learn "how to take tests"? Now that you know this book isn't just a list of tricks for psyching yourself up for exams, are you willing to put some effort into learning how to study?

GETTING THE MOST OUT OF YOUR CLASSWORK

The pattern for absorbing classroom material is: preview, view, and review.

You begin to prepare for a test when you first *view* the material in class or in your reading assignment. So your first step toward successful studying is to give yourself every chance to view the information. That means going to class with your assignments prepared so that you have a *preview* of what the class will be about.

Here are some tips on how to get the most from the classroom:

• Keep a schedule of your classes and your other activities so you can better organize your free time. Always carry a small notebook to write down your homework assignments; this way you can check quickly all the work you need to do. As soon as a report or a test is announced, note the dates for them on a calendar. Then, work backward and note the dates when you have to begin work on the report or study for the test.

• Learn to take notes. Always write down what the teacher puts on the blackboard or dictates to the class. Even when you are not required to keep a record of what goes on in class, at least jot down what topics were discussed. Note taking is a good habit to get into. The further along you get in your education, the more reliance you will have to place on your own notes, so you might as well start learning to take them efficiently. Here's how:

Always bring paper and a pencil to class. (How many

times have *you* forgotten to?) Date each page and label it with a topic word.

When taking notes, don't waste time writing complete sentences or even complete words. Use simple abbreviations, such as: +, &, ?, —, =. And since you are the only person who will have to read your notes, develop your own speedwriting symbols ("Snc u r th only prsn whl hv 2 rd yr nts, devel yr own spdrtng smbls").

Don't worry about correct form, grammar, or spelling.

Do *not* write down everything the teacher says. That's both unnecessary and physically impossible. Instead, note the main points. You will know what they are if you familiarize yourself with the general material for the course, and pay attention to clues teachers offer. For instance, if the teacher announces, "Today we will talk about X," then everything related to X is a main point. Any statement beginning with a phrase like "Remember this . . ." or "It's important . . ." is a main point. Anything written on the blackboard is a "main point." Each teacher has an individual style in giving information and with a little effort, you will soon learn how each signals the important information.

Pay attention. This will not be difficult, since one value of note taking is that it forces you to keep alert in class. Because you want to note the main points, for instance, you will find yourself trying to think ahead of the teacher a bit and asking yourself what the point is so that you can put down the most useful information.

Note any of your own ideas that the teacher's discussion may trigger. That kind of mental activity aids memory and helps to keep your attention from wandering.

Finally, always write down your assignment and any special instructions that go with it.

• As soon as possible after a class, review the notes you took during it. Studies of learning patterns show that the sooner you go over material, the better and longer you will retain it. Later review locks it in, but immediate review helps to wedge it. So, if you have time immediately, fine. If not, carve a few minutes out of the next few hours and look back at your notes. Fill in any gaps you may have left in your notebook, and mentally try to "hear" the teacher's words as you read through your summary of them. A few extra minutes now will go a long way later, when you are preparing for a quiz or an exam.

READ IT RIGHT

When you read to learn, study, and remember, you must do it differently from the way you read for fun. To retain information efficiently—to absorb the maximum amount in the shortest time, and hold onto it for the longest period—you need to follow this (not surprising) pattern: *preview, view,* and *review.*

To *preview* any book or chapter that you will be reading for school, skim it first. For a whole book, fiction or nonfiction, read through the table of contents, the chapter headings and subheadings, picture captions, charts, even the index—anything that is set apart from the text and that gives an idea of what the book is about. When you have to read a chapter in a textbook, do the same thing, and also read any of the summaries that usually precede or follow it. Read through any chapter questions that may be included, too, even if they aren't assigned, and go over any questions that your teacher may want you to answer about the reading assignment. In that way, you'll have a preview not only of what the chapter is about, but also of what you will have to get out of it.

At the *viewing* stage of reading, your goal is to get a clear idea of what the material says. That means you need to read it—and more. While you read, take notes. If you're allowed to, mark the main points in the textbook. If not, jot them down in your notebook. Work the sample problems in a math or science book. Ask yourself questions as you read. Keep in mind homework questions and those at the back of the chapter, of course, but also "question" the book. Right now, for example, the question you should be asking is, "Why question the book?" The answer: because the mental action of asking and answering helps hold the material better than the rather passive act of simply reading. Get into the habit of imagining possible test questions as you read material. For instance, you can reword "Follow this pattern: *preview, view,* and *review*" as "What pattern of studying works best to absorb and retain material?"

Since you can't retain anything you don't understand, make notes of items you find confusing while reading. Go back and try to figure them out for yourself, but if you can't, remind yourself to ask the teacher in the next class. Also, write down any words you don't know, and look up their definitions.

Reviewing is off to an easy start if you have been assigned questions to answer for homework. Read each question and go back through the chapter to find the complete answer. But whether or not you have such an assignment, you should review the reading anyway. Try the following techniques to see which help you best to remember what you read:

Reread the assignment one paragraph or section at a time. Look away from it, and summarize it *out loud.*

Write down a list of questions on the topic of the chapter, then write out your answers to them.

Make an outline of the chapter that covers the main points and all the subtopics in it.

List all key words, concepts, formulas, equations, names, and dates, and fill in all the information that pertains to them.

Note points that may be brought up in class as topics for either questions or discussions so that you will be prepared to participate.

Follow a similar procedure for an in-depth review of your day's classroom notes: Skim over them again; highlight the main points; organize them in your own fashion; recite them; ask questions (for example, "How does this tie in with what I've just read in the text assignment?").

And before you count yourself finished for the night, quickly *skim* the highlights of the notes and reading for that class since your last test. Fifteen minutes for each course per day will be enough to keep all the material fresh in your mind.

Toward Better Study Skills

All this may sound like too much work, but when you do your reading according to such an effective system, you will find that you make much better use of your time than you do when you simply read. It may take one and a half times as long, but this type of review is at least *twice* as effective, so you're actually saving time and energy.

Research has shown that the brain retains material much more effectively from frequent, brief reviews than from single long ones. Also, by making the effort to take notes and to recite out loud, you are taking an active role in your studies; and psychologists find that active review is much more valuable than passive reading. Therefore, you'll likely remember the material so well that you can cut way down on the effort and worry of studying for bigger tests and exams.

CRAMMING

Everyone faces situations for which they have to *cram* material into their heads for an exam or presentation. To prepare for these emergencies, everyone should be aware of his or her own study strengths, as outlined earlier in this chapter. Of course, the pattern of *preview, view, review* still applies, only in a more condensed form. The memory tricks described in Chapter 6 will help to concentrate the high points in the memory, and the relaxation techniques outlined in Chapter 4 will help *a lot*.

ALL WORK AND NO PLAY

Your life shouldn't be all work and no play, of course, no matter how serious a student you are. And it needn't be, if you organize your time well. Organization is perhaps even more important if you are *not* such a serious student, and when done well, it will actually allow you more time for other activities.

Start by estimating the amount of time you need to spend daily on homework for each of your courses. Your teachers should tell you how much time they expect—if they don't, ask. Add to that about fifteen minutes per course for your daily review. Include some good chunks of time every few days and on the weekend to allow for exam studying and report writing. Then consider the amount of time you spend on other activities in your life: clubs, sports, friends, household chores, or a part-time job.

Arrange all of these as best you can within the hours between your arrival home from school and your bedtime. If it's a tight squeeze, think about other pieces of time you can carve out: on rides to and from school, for instance, or during any study halls you may have. First thing in the morning is a productive study time for many people, too—and it's a good idea to spend a few morning minutes glancing over the work due for the day.

Your schedule should allow leisure for fun and friends, without wasting much time. Are there wasted hours in your day that could be used for more effective work, or for play?

If you find that you are spending all your time on work, or *much* more time than your classmates do, reconsider your schedule of classes or talk with your guidance counselor. If any one course demands much more time than others, discuss that, too. The teacher may not realize how much work other teachers give you, or it may be that you should switch to a less demanding class.

If you find that your social life, your afterschool activities, your part-time work, or all three, are taking up too much of your time, consider cutting back on them or switching some into weekend hours. These cutbacks are not only to allow you more time for studying. They also will insure that you have some private time just for yourself. This is important, because at this time of your life, you should not simply be taking care of business, but taking care of yourself, too. You should be averaging—really—eight hours of sleep a night. You should be eating three solid meals a day, plus snacks that offer nutrition rather than empty calories. And you should be getting some sort of regular, fairly vigorous exercise.

Not only will such good habits help you grow and stay healthy, but they will improve your schoolwork, too. You may have heard this so many times that it's boring, but it's true: You can't do well in school if your brain lacks the nourishment it needs or if fatigue keeps your mind from being clear or your eyes from functioning. Exercise—whether in the form of sports, jogging, walking, calisthenics, dancing, or anything that's fun and comfortable for you—actually increases your staying power day by day, and insures that the brain gets sufficient oxygen to operate. You will also find that making time for relaxation to break up your study hours will increase the effectiveness of that study.

Review your life and your priorities—your short-term goals and your long-term ones. See what you can do to keep yours in balance. This can also be a basic defense against the "nerves" that afflict many test takers.

4. Nothing to Be Afraid Of:

PSYCHING UP AND COOLING DOWN

Think about the last time you took a big test. Close your eyes, and in your mind, try to "see" the students around you. Watch that guy's knee bounce rapidly up and down, or that girl chewing her nails. One boy may be running his hands through his hair, while another keeps wiping his forehead and his glasses. The girl next to you is smiling and laughing—rather loudly—while she jiggles her pencil against her desk. Another girl is frowning as she pores over some last-minute notes. And at least one person is probably boasting about how little the exam means or how easy it will be. Some students appear calm, but they're staring, unblinking, into space.

All of these students are nervous about the impending test. Some may suffer from a more severe form of nervousness called *test anxiety*.

Now, think back to how *you* felt when you last faced an important test. Did you have trouble sleeping the night before? Did you have the slightly queasy feeling of "butterflies in the stomach"? Did you feel sweaty, or chilled, or feverish—or a little bit dizzy? Was your mouth dry, or your face twitchy? Did the slightest noise distract you from your work?

If tests make you nervous or panicky, any or all of those symptoms are probably all too familiar.

We all get tense, nervous, anxious, or even frightened when we face important tests in our lives—whether they are tests on paper, on the athletic field or stage, in a driver ed. car, or in a job interview.

Even when we try to deny that we are nervous, our bodies often give us away with physical symptoms. This is because our bodies, minds, and emotions are connected parts of a single package, and because we humans are, physically, animals. The bodies of all animals ready them to "fight or take flight" when they are threatened or frightened. So when we feel danger—even danger from an innocent-looking paper and pencil—our bodies react as if they were preparing for actual combat or escape.

Fine—nervousness, even in its severe form, is natural. The problem arises when the fear itself becomes defeating. Nerves can make it hard for you to prepare for a test, since they can hamper your mind's ability to absorb study material. A fear of tests can result in a poor performance, even when you have studied thoroughly.

Luckily, you have many ways of getting rid of that fear.

LOOKING BACK

First, it will help to understand *why* tests might make you nervous.

- You would not be reading this book if you did not take school—and the tests that go with it—seriously. You probably want to do well at this stage of your education so that you can proceed to the next level of your life, whether in school or at work. You know that test scores can make a difference, so you may get especially uptight when you confront an exam.
- Your parents may also play a part in your attitude toward tests. Whether you are a serious student or not, they may pressure you in obvious and not so obvious ways. Parents who insist that you do well in school may punish you or withhold privileges when you do poorly on tests, so even a minor one becomes a much bigger deal.

One high school boy who seemed to have everything he needed for success was terrified of tests. He was class president, an athletic hero, good looking, and popular, but even quizzes turned him to trembling jelly, because his parents never let up on their insistence that he "had to" go to a top college and "had to" get all A's. Other parents may subtly cut their kids down with comments like, "Well, next time you'll do better" when they bring home a B. Or they may reinforce a bad attitude by saying things like, "I never did well on math tests, either."

- Teachers, too, have ways of making you more frightened than you need be. In one classroom, young children were told before their first standardized achievement test: "You must do well on this test, because the scores will go into your permanent record and will stay with you for the rest of your lives." In another, they heard the explanation: "The state requires us to give you these tests, to make sure we're teaching you something; but I know that, whether or not I've taught you anything, you're all smart enough to make good scores." Which kids were more likely to develop relaxed and healthy attitudes about standardized tests?

Some teachers may use tests more as punishments than as checkups on your progress. Others may rate your test results, not with positive words that encourage you to try harder but with negative ones that just make you feel dumb. Too much of that and you come to believe that you *are* a dummy.

• Many students who are afraid of tests feel that way because they don't feel good about themselves. They may mistakenly equate doing well on tests with being a good person. Or perhaps they've had bad experiences in the past with test taking, and having failed once, they expect to fail again. Soon, they begin to feel like failures, and they are so afraid to face another bad experience that they freeze.

If you are afraid of tests, do you know why? Think for a moment about exams you have taken and the reactions of your parents, teachers, and friends to your test results. Think about ideas your family may have passed on to you. Try to remember ways in which significant teachers in your life have prepared you for important tests: Did they make you feel confident, or uptight?

Those recollections can be important clues to your attitude—and your attitude counts for a lot in success on tests and efficiency in studying.

"The only thing we have to fear is fear itself," President Franklin D. Roosevelt assured Americans during the Great Depression, and that advice applies equally to taking tests. Being afraid of a test can, by itself, make you so tense that you don't do as well as you should. You may not be able to concentrate, or your physical reactions may paralyze you. But there are very practical ways of making sure that the portrait your grades and scores present of you is accurate—or actually more flattering than reality.

PSYCHING UP

One of the most important factors in effective studying and successful test taking is a positive attitude. When you are plowing through a chapter you're likely to be tested on, do you think things like, "I'll never be able to understand this!"? This idea itself can defeat you, so focus your attention instead on taking the step-by-step approach to reading and studying outlined in the last chapter—and ask for help when you need it. You'll find that you can understand almost anything you have to.

Do you tend to remember all the times you've done badly—scored low on a test, or messed up in class? Then do this: Go back over your grades and get an accurate picture of them. A B is not as good as an A, but it's still a fine grade. A C is not so hot, until you remember how hard you tried to grasp the material in the first place. If you got marks that were nothing to be proud of at all, analyze why you did badly and think about what you would do now to do better. Did you simply not study? Well, now you will. Did you have trouble getting along with the teacher? To solve problems like that, try turning on a little charm for the sake of the cause. Did you really not understand the material? Next time, you'll know to ask for extra help. The point is: Rather than dwell on the failures, think about positive ways to avoid them in the future.

You are taking steps to improve your study skills and test scores right now—pat yourself on the back for that and for your other successes. You'll start thinking better of yourself and expecting good results. Then, through a process called the *self-fulfilling prophecy,* you will begin to do as well as you expect.

If you are shackled by serious test anxiety, you will find a technique that behavioral psychologists call *desensitization* useful. The idea is to imagine vividly situations related to test taking, starting with less scary aspects and working up to the most frightening, all the while concentrating on staying calm, breathing regularly, and keeping your muscles relaxed.

For example, you might imagine this sequence of test situations:

1. I see an article in the paper about test scores of local students.
2. A friend complains about having to study for a test.
3. On the first day of class, the teacher announces the testing schedule for the semester.
4. The teacher reminds the class about a quiz the next day.
5. The teacher pops an unannounced quiz.
6. The teacher says that the test in two weeks will count for one-third of the grade.
7. I am organizing my notes to begin studying a week before the exam.
8. Three days before the test, a classmate reminds me of material I haven't even looked at.

9. The night before the test, I lie awake trying to remember all the major points.
10. The morning of the test I'm going over notes while eating breakfast.
11. In the classroom, I overhear others taking about what and how they've studied.
12. The test papers are being handed out.
13. I look over the test and see that there are more essay questions than I had expected.
14. The person next to me has a scratchy pen that is distracting me.
15. Others seem to be writing more than I am.
16. There are two short-answer questions I can't possibly answer.
17. Others are handing in their papers and I'm not nearly done.
18. The teacher is looking at the time and straightening the desk.
19. I am turning in my test paper.
20. After the test, I'm talking it over and remembering points I didn't put down.

Now jot down your own "hierarchy" of possible threats. Close your eyes and go through it several times in your mind, noting your reactions and concentrating on controlling them and on keeping your body relaxed. Follow this procedure every so often, and you'll feel yourself growing less and less tense each time you imagine a scary scene. Then, when the event actually occurs, you will have trained yourself so that a deep breath is all that's needed to relax.

You might also find it useful to visualize happy endings: your feeling of relief when the test is done; the praise you will get for doing well; your sense of pride at having worked hard, and so on. It works!

It works in part because the physical and mental effort you take to clear your mind and relax your body will in itself counteract the fears that are causing your anxious state.

COOLING DOWN

Are tests a "headache" to you? Then your head may actually ache. Do you feel that too much responsibility "rests on your shoulders," wish that the teacher would "get off your back," or worry that your parents will "have your neck" if you don't do well? Then you may well feel special tension in those parts of your body. And you may not be talking lightly when you say that tests make you "sick to your stomach."

Remember that your mind and your body are one. Your physical well-being can be affected by your psychological attitude, and your mental state can be improved through physical means. By working to make your muscles loose and relaxed, for instance, you can ease the tension and anxiety that you feel in the pit of your stomach. Taking long walks or playing an occasional vigorous game of ball can help you unwind. Warm baths or showers help you loosen up, too.

For more thorough relaxation before you begin to study—or if you can't sleep the night before a big test—try these.

- Sit in a comfortable chair (or lie in bed if you're ready to go to sleep). Close your eyes and take a deep breath. Then, starting with your toes, slowly make every part of your body go limp. Imagine that your arms, legs, torso, and neck are like floppy rubber bands. Don't move to your leg muscles until your feet and toes are completely loose. Work your way up the rest of your body, loosening up each joint and muscle. Your face and head are especially important to loosen up. Let your jaw sag and feel your tongue loosen. Make sure that your eyes are shut gently, not squeezed together. Feel your scalp loosen under your hair. Don't move for a while—just savor the delicious feeling of being limp and unwound.

While you're studying or taking the test, tension may creep up on you without your realizing it, both because physically you're locked in one position and psychologically you may be fretting. It's important to stretch the tension out of those spots periodically.

- You can work the tension out of your neck and upper back by slowly rotating your head, first in one direction and then in the other. Rotate your shoulders, too, and feel the kinks come out. Rub your shoulder and neck muscles firmly with your fingers, and you can literally feel knotted muscles untie themselves.
- You can relax your spine by alternately curving and arching it. Sitting in your chair, or, when you can, lying on your back or kneeling on all fours, curve your back into as much of a circle as you can, by sucking in your gut and pushing your chin onto your chest. Do this very slowly, and then, just as slowly, go the other way, until your belly is out, your chin is up, and your spine is a curving arch.
- To loosen your whole body and start your circulation going, swing your arms in an S-shaped motion and your legs and torso around in huge, loose circles. Stretch your head

and arms up tall and tight, then let yourself droop into a sag, with your head hanging limp. Repeat several times, inhaling deeply as you stretch up, and exhaling as you sag down.

You can and should do miniversions of those stretches before and during an exam, and you can even do a form of the following total relaxer while you're sitting in the testing room:
- Tense every muscle in your body as tightly as you can and hold for a count of ten. Then, one by one, relax those muscles. Concentrate on breathing regularly and deeply. Close your eyes and listen to your breathing.

Or close your eyes and concentrate on creating a visual image of something soothing—a meadow scene, perhaps, with butterflies, or a dark velvet curtain with a single feather floating down in front of it. Focus on feeling how peaceful the vision is, and you will soon feel peaceful and relaxed yourself.

A little bit of tension is probably useful when you face a test, but it should be a positive feeling—excitement rather than anxiety, a slightly keyed-up feeling that comes from wanting to do well rather than fearing doing badly. Think of the difference between the excitement you feel while watching your favorite sports team play or watching an adventure movie, and the nervousness you'd experience if you were actually on the field or in the middle of that dangerous adventure.

No matter how much pressure you're under at exam time, or no matter how nervous you may be, make sure to allow time for breaks and relaxation. Try to get your usual amount of sleep and to eat well and exercise regularly, since the brain and hands that are going to work on that exam need to be in good shape. Some students throw their whole lives out of whack while studying for exams by staying up all night, skipping meals or gorging on low-nutrition snack foods, and getting generally goofy. Those extremes are self-defeating, but a little bit of special treatment during exam time can lighten your mood and remind your subconscious that you *are* in high gear, so indulge yourself with some breaks in routine, and plan for a party or a spree after exams are over.

Don't keep cramming the night before and the morning of an exam. Just do a quick review to refresh your memory. Eat your normal breakfast, and think positive! Right before the test, stay away from huddles with your classmates. Their information or misinformation will just be confusing, and their nervousness might be catching.

Laughter, though, can work wonders, for both physical and psychological states. I failed my driving test three times because my accelerator foot was trembling with tension. Finally I got a tester who made a joke just as I was starting the car, and the rest was a relaxed breeze. So if you do talk with your fellow testers, keep it light and joking.

Take a deep breath as you take your seat, smile at someone, and make yourself comfortable.

Section Two:
The Tests

5. The "Small Stuff":

QUIZZES AND TESTS—
AND THE FORMS THEY TAKE

"Me? I'm always comfortable when I take a test—I really am." This college freshman is telling the truth, and she gets A's and B's in four out of her five courses. She's not doing so well in the fifth, but she knows she can repeat the course if necessary, and now knows how to deal with those tests the next time. Not everyone has that kind of freedom, but the attitude, at any rate, is healthy. She knows that tests are important in her life, but that they need not control it.

You will be less likely to get uncomfortable about tests if you know fully how to cope with each type you are most likely to encounter. The chapters in this section will cover the *what* and the *why* as well as the *how* of dealing with various kinds of tests, because an understanding of the background will help you develop your techniques.

This chapter starts with quizzes because, as you probably know, they are *not* such small stuff.

The "Small Stuff"

First of all, bigger exams are comprised of several or all of the forms of questions that you find on quizzes, in order to get at a lot of information from as many different angles as possible. Secondly, they can be as much of an agony as the bigger tests if you don't know how to approach them. And finally, quizzes are useful not only for the teacher, but for you, too.

WHY BOTHER?

Teachers do have reasons for presenting you with this small stuff, of course. Quizzes and periodic tests are, ideally, a way to check on students' progress in a given course. If you consistently do poorly on these tests, it may mean that, for some reason, you are not learning what the course is teaching. If an entire class does poorly on test after test, it can be a sign that the teacher is not doing his or her job well enough, either in not getting the message across or in not designing the tests properly.

A good teacher with enough time and patience will pick up these clues. He may try to pinpoint the student's trouble and offer extra help. She may take a close look at her teaching method and adapt it to the needs of that class, or rethink the design of her tests.

As a more practical matter, classroom tests help teachers determine students' grades for the course. Class participation, homework production, and work on special projects should always be a part of your grade, of course, but tests are a fairly clear-cut way to rate performance. Usually, teachers will count tests as about one-third of the final grade, with quizzes counting for less than larger exams. Some teachers, however, have been known to overweight test grades, even going so far as to hinge the entire grade on the final exam result.

Although it is usually not good teaching practice, it sometimes happens that teachers use tests as part of discipline, to keep a class in line. This may be justifiable when a teacher realizes that a class is not buckling down to work, and introduces a regular series of quizzes to get it in shape. But when the sudden announcement of a test replaces the good control a teacher should have in a classroom, it serves little purpose. That may be all well and good, but . . .

WHAT'S IN IT FOR YOU?

Believe it or not, you have a lot, besides annoyance, to gain from "minor" tests.

• They can let *you* know how you're doing. If you get a low grade on a couple of quizzes, even though you think you've been paying attention and you've made an attempt to study, either you may not understand the course work, or you may not be studying properly. And you're better off knowing early that you have to shape up. Otherwise, you'll be up a creek when the final exam comes around.

• They give you a chance to get a feel for the teacher's approach to tests. Most teachers have their own styles of designing and grading tests. As you work on the less important ones, you'll become familiar with the pattern that you can expect on the bigger deals.

• They can actually make your life easier. Quizzes force you to study the course material in little bits, every so often. In this way, you will have the information more firmly in your mind by the time a more important test comes. And if you're nervous about taking tests in the first place, you can view the quizzes as practice, giving you a chance to work off your nerves early on.

- They can be an easy way to establish a good image. Whether they admit it or not, whether they even realize it or not, teachers often form an impression in their minds of the performance levels of individual students, and may read their work accordingly as the school year goes on. If you take early quizzes and small tests seriously, you may create a situation in which the teacher, seeing your name on a more important test paper, will assume you will do well, and grade accordingly. Since you have less preparation to do for quizzes than for bigger tests, you may have an easy "in" to the teacher's good graces.

- And if you do badly on one of those quizzes? Then go to the teacher and review the problems you had with the test. Your serious intention will at least make a good impression. Even if you want to protest an unfair test or an inaccurate grade, when you do so politely, you will show that you are sincere about the importance of the course.

Every test, big or small, has something in it for you. Each one, handled the right way, will help you learn something about yourself, about your teachers, or about the test-taking process itself.

ASKING THE RIGHT QUESTIONS

Whether you are preparing for a quiz or for a standardized test, the first step is to ask questions:

- Find out as much about the quizzes as you can, and as

far in advance as possible. At the beginning of each course, teachers should announce their testing policies. Can you expect a quiz each week on a given day? Should you be prepared for surprise quizzes? How often, if ever, will you have review tests—after each section covered, or only once before the final exam? What form will the quizzes usually take? If the teacher does not give this information, *ask*.

- Ask about the grading system, and how the overall grade is broken down, because this will influence how you allocate your study time for the course and how you divide your efforts on each quiz and test given. See pages 77–79 for an explanation of how teachers arrive at test grades by different systems.
- Ask when the teacher has scheduled time to help you go over material you don't understand, because the key to doing well on quizzes is to keep up with the classwork and homework. Good teachers plan instruction so that each part of a course ties up logically with the next and give homework assignments that will help you get the most out of all the work you do. *If* you do the work, you will almost automatically be prepared for quizzes. And if you have any area of difficulty, ask about it right away so that you don't fall behind.

Even on days when you don't have an assignment in a given class, remember that you *do* have an assignment: to *review*. If you skim over the course material lightly each day, not only will you be prepared for any unannounced quizzes the teacher springs on you, but you also will make a habit of the most important study skill there is.

THE FORMS TESTS TAKE

For even the smallest of quizzes, your basic strategy should be that outlined in Chapter 2: to *preview* the instructions and the entire test; to work the test carefully, starting with the easier items; and to *review* your answers for clarity and accuracy.

However, the specific form that each quiz or test will take makes a difference, too. At this point, then, it's important to look closely at the various forms of tests and your strategies for dealing with each of them.

Quizzes may consist of any one of these types of tests. Here are some hints for tackling each kind.

Short-Answer Tests

LISTS TO DEFINE OR IDENTIFY

Define the following words:

1. test _____
2. grade _____
3. review _____
4. guess _____
5. try _____
6. numbered _____
7. standardized _____
8. scale _____

- Answer grammatically, if possible. For instance, in number 2 of this sample, "to rate performance" is a better answer than "when the teacher marks a test." Spelling counts, too! You may lose out on number 1 if you write "examinashun" instead of "examination."
- Answer within the context of the course. To define "scale" (number 8) as "a mechanical device for weighing objects" might be fine for a science course, but for a course in testing it wouldn't count for much.
- The more you can use the exact words given by the teacher or the textbook, the better off you are, since that's what the teacher is looking for.
- When you are stumped for an exact answer, at least try to write down an example. For number 7, you might not get full credit for "The SAT is an example of a standardized test," but you would probably get some.
- If you have the time, beef up your definitions with examples or details. "To see or go over again" is a good definition for number 3, but you might pick up extra points if you add something like, "It is the third step in studying and in taking an exam," or "Immediate review will help fix course material in the mind."

FILL-IN-THE-BLANKS

Complete the following sentences:

1. Some of the people who object to testing procedures are _____.

2. Those who know how to take tests often find them _____.

The "Small Stuff"

3. Among the tests that can have the biggest influence on your life are those that we call _____.

4. Since you are reading this book, you probably take tests _____.

5. Students who have scored significantly higher on previous exams find that when they face a new one, they feel _____.

6. You are probably reading this book because you are _____ about taking tests.

7. Students who know how to take tests are called _____.

8. The best pattern to follow for studying and test-taking is preview, _____, review.

9. Section II of this book details hints about taking each type of _____.

- Look for clues within the grammar of the sentence. For item 1, "me" would obviously be wrong, because the answer has to be in the plural.
- Use your common sense. The answer for number 6 would *not* be "confident," since that doesn't make sense.
- Choose the best word. "Hard" might fit as an answer to number 3, but it has a lot less value than "standardized."
- If the blanks are of markedly different size, or if some items have spaces between two or more blanks, use this as a clue. In number 9, the best answer is more likely to be "test" than "examination," since the blank is short. But beware: Most teachers try to make the blanks of uniform size, so you can't always count on that for a clue.

- Read through each sentence to be sure it makes sense the way you have completed it.
- Again, always answer within the context of the course, using the exact word given by the teacher or the textbook whenever possible.

MATCHING TESTS

Match the phrases in column B with the words from column A that best fit the meaning.

A	B
test	To make an effort
exam	To assist
grade	Evaluation
score	To prepare for an examination
practice	Rank
study	To be concerned
try	In sequence
worry	
help	
fret	
aid	
paper	
numbered	
order	
preview	
scale	
guess	

- Work from the longer column to the shorter one. Looking at the word "test," for instance, you have fewer possibili-

The "Small Stuff"

ties to choose from than you would have if you had started with the word "evaluation."
- Don't match anything you're not sure of.
- If you're not sure whether all items must be matched, ask.

TRUE-FALSE TESTS

Indicate whether the following statements are true or false.

		True	False
1.	All students find exams difficult.	____	____
2.	A quiz is less likely to be important for a student's grade than a midterm exam.	____	____
3.	Clues to the answer are never given in the question.	____	____
4.	Test takers can expect true-false answers to follow a regular pattern, such as T F F T F.	____	____
5.	The true-false part of a test is always counted as the least important.	____	____
6.	Smart students do well on tests, because they cheat.	____	____
7.	A course in study skills is an important part of all school programs.	____	____
8.	Tests never scare some people.	____	____
9.	This book guarantees you an A on every test.	____	____
10.	Nobody feels that tests are fair.	____	____

- Look carefully at the qualifying words: absolute words usually point to a "false," since few facts are absolute. In item 1, for instance, the word "all" makes the statement false. But the rule itself is not absolute: item 8 is true despite its "never" because of that "some."
- Does the statement have any false parts? Number 6 begins as a true statement, but is false because of its second half.
- Do *not* look for patterns. Teachers work hard to avoid patterns, and if there's a regular one, it's probably accidental, so don't take the chance. You *can* generally figure that the "trues" and "falses" will be about evenly balanced, however (with a tendency for more "trues," if anything), so if the answers you've marked are heavily one or the other, you have a chance of being right if you fill in your blanks with the opposite answer.
- Unless you've been told not to, guess at answers that you aren't sure of. (If you are penalized for wrong answers, don't guess.) Since you have only two possibilities in a true-false test, you have a 50-50 chance of being right, so guessing here is safer than in other forms of tests.

Multiple-Choice Tests

Circle the answer that best completes the statement.

1. Multiple-choice tests are _____ common type of exam.
   - a. many
   - b. simple
   - c. one
   - d. NONE OF THE ABOVE

The "Small Stuff"

2. You must be _____ when answering a multiple-choice question.
   a. careful
   b. relaxed
   c. right
   d. ALL OF THE ABOVE

3. Multiple-choice questions are _____ scored with the same weight as other types of questions.
   a. never
   b. always
   c. sometimes
   d. ALL OF THE ABOVE

4. When working a multiple-choice question, you should _____ the possible answers first.
   a. read
   b. mark
   c. ignore
   d. NONE OF THE ABOVE

5. A multiple-choice test is not the _____ type of exam that requires reviewing.
   a. best
   b. only
   c. LEAVE BLANK
   d. NONE OF THE ABOVE

- Multiple-choice questions are similar to true-false questions, but they have more choices than two, so look for absolutes in the answers just as you would in true-false statements. (See item 3, for example.)
- Skim through the question first to see if you can answer it on your own. Then see if you can find an option close to

your own answer. In item 1, for instance, a good guess might be the word "a". Among the options, the word "one" is closest.

- If you don't immediately know an answer, eliminate the options that you know cannot be right. In item 5, option d cannot be right, so you are left with only three from which to choose.
- Look for clues in grammar and sense. Option a in item 5 does not really make grammatical or logical sense in the sentence, so you can eliminate that one, too.
- Once you have narrowed the choices to two, you are fairly safe in guessing, *unless* the test is one in which wrong answers are deducted from right ones.
- If necessary, work backwards: Try each of the answers and see which one fits best. By using this system, you would find that option d is the best answer for item 2.
- Remember that you are looking for the best answer from among your choices. You may be able to think up a "righter" answer, but you have only a limited selection of choices.

Problem-Solving Tests

Solve the following problems:

1. Define the area of this triangle:

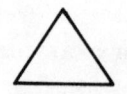

The "Small Stuff"

2. Find the square root:

    3   45   67

3. Find x: 37x = 42+5

4. 82
   ×7
   ‾‾

5. ½ + ¼ = _____

6. 3/4 − 2/8 = _____

7. ¼ × ¼ = _____

8. 5/10 ÷ 3/12 = _____

9. What is the next number in this sequence:
   1/10, 2/10, 3/10, 4/10, _____

• Read the problem carefully to be sure you know what it is asking. You'll get item 5 wrong if you subtract instead of add. Or if you are asked to find the sum, don't multiply!

• Reread the problem to get the facts you need for your work. Write them down and start to work the problem.

• On multiple-choice problems, make a rough estimate first and see if any of your options come close.

• Check your answer by working backwards. In item 4, you would learn that 573 was the wrong answer if you divided 573 by 7.

• Watch for careless errors! You might feel that a long series of equations is a snap, but if, in the middle of the problem, you add where you should subtract, you will get the wrong answer.

Essay Questions

Answer three of the following questions:

1. Define what is meant by being testwise in terms of the intelligence of the test taker, the ability to read instructions, and the approach to the test itself.

2. Outline the best procedure for studying and for taking tests.

3. Compare and contrast the difference between the way you take tests and the way the testwise student does.

4. Explain why you are reading this book.

5. Define the difference between this test-taking guide and others, comparing and contrasting the contents of the two types by describing both. Evaluate both types, supporting your argument with a detailed example chosen from each. Summarize your response in outline form.

The "Small Stuff"

- If you have a choice among several questions to answer, read through all of them quickly to decide which to select.
- Then read the questions you choose carefully, looking for the key words that will tell you what is wanted in your essay. (In item 2, the key word is "outline.") Be sure you understand what the common key words mean. You will find a list of definitions, with examples, on pages 71–77.
- Budget your time: How many questions do you have to answer, and how long do you have for doing them? The sample has five questions. A typical class hour is fifty minutes, which means that if you are instructed to answer all five questions, you would have ten minutes for each. You might know more about some questions than about others and so will need time to write more facts, but the ones that are harder will take added thinking time, so it balances out. You also should allow some time for organizing your thoughts. (To get your thoughts organized, pretend that you are the teacher, standing before the class and ticking off on your fingers the most important points.)
- Jot down all of your ideas quickly, and arrange them in a rough outline form. It would be a good idea to do this for all of the questions before you start to answer any of them fully, for two reasons: This really starts your mind working on all the responses, and you will always have something down on paper even if time runs out. But if you're like me and feel more comfortable about concentrating on one set of ideas at a time, then take each question individually.
- Where possible, use the question as the basis for your outline. The essay for item 1, for instance, would deal first with "intelligence," then with "ability," and finally with "approach."

- Plan to write as though *you* were the teacher, or as though you were trying to teach something to another person, rather than to show off all that you know. This approach gives you two advantages: It will make your answer more forceful and convincing, since you are, in effect, playing the role of the person with the knowledge; and, if you use your own teacher as a model, it will likely produce the kind of answer that the teacher might like best. (On question 2, for example, you would do well to answer according to the advice given in this book, whether you think it is "best" or not.)
- Try to compose a beginning, a middle, and an end. At the very least, your lead should be a topic sentence taken from the question. The lead for number 3 might be "There are many differences between the way I take tests and the way a testwise student does." Close with at least a short summary, for example, "To summarize, it is far better to be testwise."
- Give as many appropriate details as possible. "Because I want to" would be a poor answer for item 4. The more dates, places, and facts you can put in to back up your general statements, the better your score will be. This does *not* mean you should include everything you know about anything. Few teachers will be fooled by a long answer that is filled with facts that have little or nothing to do with the question at hand. On item 3, for instance, if you are not sure about how you take tests and have no idea about how testwise students go about it, you may be tempted to write an essay on how you feel about tests. That would not answer the question, any more than would a list of prices for rutabagas at local grocery stores.
- However, you may get away with a few points for a

baffling essay if you work more subtly at changing the subject. An "ignorant" answer might gain some points (at least from a grader with a sense of humor) if you wrote a lead like "The way I take tests gets low grades; testwise students have systems that get higher grades . . . Testwise students, however, tend to be people who are unlikeable—unlikeable in the sense that . . ."

More seriously, suppose that the question is, "Compare the discovery of America with the first landing on the moon," and you haven't studied what you should have about the discovery of America or are at a loss to describe the first landing on the moon. You might begin with a statement like, "New discoveries are always a venture into the unknown. Like Columbus, the American astronauts had no idea of what to expect when they opened the door of their spacecraft . . ." and then proceed with a detailed discussion of whichever part of the comparison—Columbus or the astronauts—you do know about.

- When you are *not* sure about a fact, qualify it. The phrase "around the middle of the 19th century" will give you more credit than "1848" if the year was actually 1849.
- Use the best grammar and spelling you can, and write clearly!
- If you run short of time, note that fact on your paper and finish your essay in quick outline form.
- However you manage it, always write *something!*

Key Words Used in Essay Questions

Here is a list of the key words that you are likely to encounter in an essay test, as well as an explanation of what they mean and examples of how to approach answering them.

analyze: Break down a whole into the parts that make it up. "Analyze the characteristics that make dogs valuable to humans." Dogs are trainable for a variety of purposes ... They display loyalty, affection, and dependency ...

compare: Find resemblances and differences between qualities and characteristics of two or more items, stressing similarities.
"Compare dogs with cats." Both are four-legged mammals, both are domesticated breeds of wild animals now commonly found as house pets ...

contrast: Examine associated items with an eye toward explaining differences and dissimilarities.
"Contrast dogs with cats." Dogs are found in a wider range of sizes than cats; dogs bark and cats meow ...

criticize: Express your judgment in evaluating the worth, accuracy, or significance of the topic presented. Back up your opinion with analysis and explanation.
"Criticize dogs as pets." Dogs can be a messy, sometimes dangerous, inconvenience because they are difficult to housebreak, chew up household items, shed hair, and may bite or attack—while requiring daily feeding and exercise.

define: Give brief, clear meanings for words or concepts. If necessary, differentiate them from related items and set them in an appropriate context. It is best to use parallel grammar in definitions (in other words, use a noun phrase to define a noun, a verb for a verb, and so on), and never use the word to be defined as part of the definition, unless as an example of its use.

The "Small Stuff" 73

"Define dog" (for a biology course). A four-legged carnivorous mammal of the family Canidae.

"Define dog" (for a social studies course). One of the earliest known domesticated animals, a descendant of wolves tamed far back in prehistoric times and continuously bred to serve humans as companions, protectors, hunters, and laborers.

describe: Discuss the topic in accurate and fine detail; give facts, not opinions.

"Describe the Cheshire Cat." The Cheshire Cat looked like many other cats when it was visible, with four legs, soft fur, whiskers, and a tail, but it could grow invisible, and in the process, sometimes all that could be seen was its head, or a wide, grinning smile.

diagram: Make a drawing and label it.

"Diagram a cat."

[Drawing of a cat with labels: EARS, WHISKERS, TAIL, BODY, LEGS, PAWS]

discuss: Analyze a topic carefully; present background, significance, and pros and cons. Back each statement with as much detail as possible.

"Discuss the human domestication of wild animals." When humans finally tamed animals for their own use, during prehistoric times, they were able for the first time to rely for food on sources other than just hunting or foraging . . .

enumerate: Make a list of topics or items. Focus on "what," "where," "who," or "when."

"Enumerate the types of domesticated animals." dog, cat, sheep, cow, horse, pig . . .

evaluate: Rate or weight the significance of the topic, appraising it and giving both pros and cons on the basis of expert sources and your own opinion. Come to a conclusion.

"Evaluate the human tendency of keeping pets." Psychologists find that pets can be of benefit to people, especially those who are lonely, by providing companionship and a reason for living. It has been shown, for instance, that the death rate of the elderly who are separated from their pets shows a sharp increase. However, pets are often kept for cruel reasons . . .

explain: Answer the questions "how" and "why" about a given topic. Interpret the facts you present and give causes for them.

"Explain the affinity between people and pets." For emotional satisfaction, people need attachments and a feeling of worth. Pets offer both, because . . .

illustrate: Explain a concept or topic with a drawing, a graph, a diagram, or written specific examples.

"Illustrate the people-pet connection in popular culture." We see the connection in such comic strips as "Peanuts," "Garfield," and "Little Orphan Annie," where the animals have at least as much importance as the people . . .

interpret: Similar to "explain," but with an emphasis on presenting examples and judgments.

The "Small Stuff"   75

"Interpret the role of the dog in *The Wizard of Oz.*" Without Toto, the plot of the story would not have gone far, since Dorothy stayed out of the storm cellar to save him. The "Oz" part of the story, too, would have made little sense had not the Wicked Witch resembled the woman who dognapped Toto. Also . . .

justify: Present arguments or sound explanations for statements or events.

"Justify the neutering of pet animals." So many kittens and puppies are born that many become unwanted and must be killed or abandoned. Also, too-frequent pregnancies sap the health of adult females, so . . .

list: As with "enumeration," itemize answers concisely.

"List the most common names of pet dogs." Rover, Fido, Rex, King, Fifi, George . . .

outline: Organize your answer in such a way that the subtopics or backup information are listed concisely under appropriate main-topic heads. This is also the key word for many types of answers: whether analyzing, comparing, contrasting, criticizing, defining, describing, evaluating, interpreting, or the like, you should gather your information and answer in a systematic progression of facts.

"In outline form, describe a cat."

1. Biological
   a. . . .
   b. . . .
   c. . . .

2. Historic
   a. . . .
   b. . . .
   c. . . .
3. Cultural
   a. . . .
   b. . . .
   c. . . .

prove: In math or science, such an instruction requires the solving of a problem, usually backed up by figures or formulas. In other areas, positive backup must come from logical reasoning or the presentation of experimental evidence.

"Prove that A = B, where A is the area of a circle. B = pi $\times$ r^2."

"Prove that both dogs and cats are mammals." Both dogs and cats are fur-bearing animals that produce live young and nurture them in infancy through the mammary glands.

relate: Show the connections or associations between or among the topics given.

"Relate the needs of humans to the needs of domesticated animals." Domesticated animals, whether dogs, cows, cats, or pigs, need care and feeding, and people need the animals for a variety of purposes. To satisfy both needs, people care for animals, and in return . . .

review: Enumerate and analyze, with some discussion, the major points of the topic presented—an examination that provides more detail than a list but less analysis than an evaluation.

The "Small Stuff"

"Review the main points recommended by this study guide." *Preview*—look over the material in advance; *view*—work on it carefully; *review*—go back and sum it up.

state: Present the main points relating to the given topic clearly and briefly, without description or argumentation.
"State the nature of test anxiety." A physical reaction triggered by a strong psychological and emotional negative reaction to tests, caused by . . .

summarize: Condense the main points, facts, or themes relating to a given topic. Similar to an outline, though not in outline form.
"Summarize the antidotes to test anxiety." Study by effective means to produce confidence. Practice relaxation techniques such as . . .

trace: Describe the development, progress, or sequence from the original point to the point asked for.
"Trace the development of standardized tests from their inception to present times." Standardized tests were made necessary by the expansion of education. They were made possible by the development of psychological measurements. In the early part of the twentieth century, and through the middle of it, they were regarded as absolutely scientifically valuable. Today, however . . .

WHERE GRADES COME FROM

The way in which tests are marked is almost as important to understand as the forms tests take. It can be especially useful to get a clear picture of how the paper will be graded *before* taking any quiz or test. Knowing how many points each question is worth and how your grade will be assigned, for instance, will make a difference in the way you approach each question. On tests that combine essays with short-answer questions, the essays usually count for more; but you will usually get some credit for even a partial answer to an essay, since the teacher is looking for a certain number of topical points and may give you credit for the ones you do make.

Some teachers—and some standardized tests—will subtract extra points for each wrong answer. For example, if you got one out of ten questions wrong, and each right answer counted 10 points, you wouldn't get a 90, but an 88, because the wrong answer counted against you for an extra 2 points. If you *skipped* the answer you got wrong, you would have gotten a 90. Since guessing is not a good idea on that kind of test, it's important to know about the grading system ahead of time.

Some tests have a maximum score of 100%, with the weight of all of the items totalling that number. Others—particularly those containing mathematical problems—assign a certain number of points to each question, no matter what those points add up to.

It can be important to know whether all the items carry equal weight, and whether you get some credit for a partial answer. For instance, if you can't, or don't have time to finish a formula or math problem, is it worth taking the time to put anything down? Some teachers will give you a few points if you show that you know how to arrive at an answer.

A test might have extra-credit questions or problems. Before spending time on them, find out two things: if your score will be *lowered* (rather than remain unchanged) for errors on

The "Small Stuff"

extra-credit items; and if you get any extra points for those items if you do well on them without completing the regular part of the test, too.

When teachers (and exam publishers) score tests, they first come up with a "raw score." On a classroom test, this might be the 88 points accumulated by your correct answers. Sometimes, this may be recorded in the teacher's book as the grade you get for the test. Or the teacher might translate that raw score into a letter or word grade: an 88 might be a B or a "Very Good!"

This translation might be done either in absolute terms or according to a "curve," or averaging system. With the absolute system, a teacher, a school, or an entire school system or testing operation uses a standard formula, such as 95–100 is A; 90–95 is A−; 85–90 is B, and so forth. When your test is graded according to a curve, on the other hand, you score not only according to your own performance but also in relationship to the rest of the test takers. With a curve, all of the raw scores can be plotted on a piece of graph paper, the lowest at one point, the highest at another, and the middle in between, with a curving line connecting those points. On a test where 100 is the perfect score, for instance, you could get an A with only a 70 if 70 was the highest score anyone in the class achieved.

How your score is translated may not be important before you take a quiz or test, but when you get the graded paper back, you need to understand not only why, but how you got the score you did because each score, even for a quiz, can be important as part of your overall school success.

A grade becomes even more significant, of course, when it comes attached to one of a course's bigger deals.

6. Bigger Deals:

COURSE EXAMS AND
HOW TO PREPARE FOR EACH TYPE

Teachers schedule midterm and final exams to find out if you've learned what you were supposed to have learned during a course or a section of it. Exams provide teachers with a good way of determining your grade for the class. They force you to study so you retain that knowledge, and they also help keep your mind on your work—hearing "You'd better stop talking; this might be on the exam" is an excellent way to get your attention!

Like quizzes, these big deals can be good for you, too. Some junior high and high schools don't use midterms and finals. "Lucky!" you might think—but that's not necessarily so. At some point in your future, whether it's in college, in a technical school, or when you want to get a license to enter a particular trade or profession, you are going to have to take some big tests, and they'll be much easier to deal with if you've had experience.

Often, students who switch from an examless school to one

that requires major examinations will complain that they wished they'd been forced to learn earlier how to take an exam. In some cases, schools have introduced finals or reinstated them so their graduates will gain experience in testing and so be better prepared in the future. The best way to develop those special test-taking skills is to take a lot of tests. People who face the last-minute panic that big exams bring on, and then learn that they can cope well despite their apprehension, aren't so panicky the next time.

HOW TO COPE

Of course, all of that wisdom assumes that you will be able to cope and that you will do well on all those tests that are so "good for you." One way to do so is to avoid that last-minute panic. And to do that:

• Start preparing for the final exam on the first day of class. This isn't as terrible as it sounds. All it means is that you do what previous chapters have outlined:

Ask if there is going to be a midterm or final exam.

Review your work every day so that it has time to sink in gradually. This way, you won't have to cram in all the material at the last minute.

Pay attention to the smaller classroom tests you take so that you get a feel for the teacher's approach to tests.

Go over with the teacher any quizzes or tests you do badly on, so that you don't make the same mistakes twice.

Ask for help with any material that causes you trouble, so that you won't get stuck the night before the exam.

- Study for the right test. This may sound silly, but it's not. Many students fail to ask the teacher what material the exam will and will not cover, so they waste their time rereading notes and texts that aren't directly related. Or they concentrate on only one portion of the course work, forgetting that a final exam will likely cover everything learned from Day One. (But remember that teachers can get quite irritated if, every time your hand goes up, it signals a "Will-this-be-on-the-exam?" question, so you'd be wise to wait until just before you're ready to begin your final studying to ask for details.)

The form of the exam, too, will make a big difference in how you study, so find out if you can expect true-false questions, multiple-choice, short answers, essays, or a combination. If it will be a combination, ask which part will carry the heaviest weight.

- Organize your study time. Plan ahead, so that for a few weeks before your big exams you'll know you have the extra time to spend reviewing. Write out a schedule, or make notes on a calendar, so you won't be too tempted to avoid the situation. Allow the most time for work on your weakest courses. If you enjoy English and it comes naturally, but you can't remember French verbs for the life of you, concentrate on French and just review the English. Within each course, as well, spend the most time on the parts that are hardest for you. Be sure you gather together all the material from each class—notes, lab work, early tests, and homework, as well as your texts and other reading material.

Get together with friends who are also serious about doing well on exams and study jointly. You might even try to find

Bigger Deals

conscientious studymates who are strong in the areas where you're weak. Go over notes and assignments, to be sure you don't have any gaps. Work together to figure out points you don't understand, and quiz each other.

BUCKLE DOWN

You, of course, are ultimately responsible for your own studying. There's no need for panic, though, because all you're going to do is follow your review pattern in a more concentrated form.

• Organize your material. For example, in the previous weeks or months, you may have covered major topics A, B, C, and D. Clip together your notes, study outlines, homework papers, and quizzes for each topic, and use slips of paper to mark your text or other reading books by topic. Plan to study each topic separately. Not only does breaking up the chunk make the job seem smaller, but your brain won't get as exhausted as it would if you plowed through the whole mass at once. You will learn and remember more from several short sessions on specific subjects than from one long, broad one.

You are better off starting with the *middle* sections (in this case, topics B and C) because people have a proven tendency to remember beginnings and endings more readily than middles.

• *Preview, view,* and *review.* For each section, glance through all the material, letting it jog your memory. (If you have been reviewing regularly all along, you may be surprised at how much you remember.) But that is not enough.

Educational experts and expert test takers say that you have to *overlearn*—you have to be able to recite the material almost without thinking—if only to give yourself the important feeling of confidence that you *know* you know it.

Don't just keep rereading all your notes and assignments, though, since that will just confuse and overload you. Instead, as you go through each section, stop periodically to recite *out loud* the main points you've just covered, as much from memory as possible. After reading through all of one section, skimming the whole thing if necessary or just your highlighted notes, begin to boil it down and summarize it—in outline form, as diagrams, into a tape recorder, however you are comfortable. If you get stumped, go back to your notes; but keep at it, putting the information into your own words. What you are doing is using your eyes, ears, voice, and hands as multiple pathways to get the information into your brain. Then, once or twice a day, go through these outlines and lists and continue to recite and review them out loud whenever possible.

• Practice. Using old tests, questions from the textbook and from homework assignments, or—even better—questions that you've made up while thinking about the test work, give yourself an exam. Write the questions out, and then write your answers, pulling in as many facts for each as you can. Or exchange tests with your friends for practice. When you do run through such an exam, do it under exam conditions: turn off the radio, TV, and stereo, clear your desk or table, and start with a fresh, blank piece of paper. (Many people can study when slouched in a chair listening to the stereo, but they blank out when bleaker, quieter surroundings say "TEST!"). After you've finished the exam,

correct it—go back over your notes and texts to check for accuracy and thoroughness.
- Prepare for the right kind of exam!

For an *essay,* make up questions that, on the basis of earlier tests and points emphasized by the teacher, you can predict are likely to be on the exam. Write out answers without referring to notes and within a time limit similar to the one you will probably have on the actual test. Jot down a rough outline and fill in as much detail as you can. Memorize the outlines for the most likely essay questions. (The tips and techniques on pages 87–91 should help with your memorization.) And be sure you know how to spell the important words that you are likely to need.

Don't imagine that just because essay questions allow some room for individuality or fudging, you can get away with learning only generalities. The more relevant names, dates, places, formulas, or other facts you can squeeze into your essays, the better your answer will look. Such readily available detail is also useful if you have to finish your exam essay in outline form; and just in case you run into an essay on the test that you feel very fuzzy about, the more hard facts you have stored in your mind, the more success you'll have at changing the subject while still showing that you know *something.*

For *short-answer* questions, you will definitely need to know all those nitty-gritty facts cold, so make lists of all the necessary details and memorize and recite them, stressing those the teacher has stressed. Boil down your notes into a tight little lump so that you can concentrate on the hard core of facts and key words. Although each type of short-answer test contains clues within it to the right answer (see pages 59–64), the colder you know your facts, the more quickly you will be able to answer—and on an exam, you won't want to waste time.

Since it is hard to make up short-answer tests for yourself, have someone drill you. Take turns with a classmate putting the facts in true-false or sentence-completion form. Or have someone in your family go through your lists, asking for definitions and explanations of each term until you can answer almost without thinking. Review and restudy the parts you have a hard time with.

The best way to study for *problem-solving* exams for math or science courses, for example, is to practice, practice, practice! Once you've got a good handle on the basic information you'll need—theories, principles, and so forth—work as many problems as you can find. Rework ones from earlier quizzes, tests, and homework; work unassigned ones in the textbook; have someone make up new problems for you. Be sure that you can understand each type of problem you will be tested on so that, for instance, no matter what the numbers involved, you will be able to recognize a time and motion problem or an energy-conversion problem and get to work on it without giving it a second thought.

The same advice applies to *language* course exams, whether English or foreign-language grammar and usage (as opposed to literature). Grammar is, after all, like math or chemistry, only it uses words instead of numbers. Know your "formulas"—the grammar rules—cold, and practice working "problems" with all the parts of speech you are required to have learned.

For *open-book* or *take-home* exams, you won't need to study and memorize quite so thoroughly, but preparation is still important, especially since grading is likely to be more stringent for these than for a memory test. Before an open-book exam, you'll want to read the material more carefully than you would for a simple class discussion; and be sure that you've marked the key points in your text. If the teacher permits you to use notes and other materials for the test, make sure you have them organized in the same logical way you would if you'd studied for a regular exam so that they're handy for your answers.

For a take-home test, be sure to follow the rules the teacher lays out: to answer in your own words, for instance, or to use only the material prescribed as sources (when you break those rules, it will be obvious on your paper). And don't make the mistake one eighth-grader did for his first take-home: he felt so casual about it that he forgot to bring the book home from school.

The better prepared you are for any type of test, the more confident you will be going into it.

MAKE YOUR MEMORY WORK

For some courses, you will have to memorize specific items—formulas, equations, word spellings, or dates, for instance. But it doesn't hurt to memorize material from any course, since the more you can put down on the exam paper, the better you will look. Also, the more material you have ready at the front of your mind, the more quickly you'll be able to get through the test.

We have two types of memory, *short term* and *long term.* Short-term memory lasts about as long as it takes to look up a phone number and dial it; long-term memory lasts indefinitely, but it often needs to be triggered. When memorizing for an exam, you need to transfer items from the short-term department into the long-term memory bank. Since most people can remember only seven or so "bits" of short-term information at a time, the first trick is, obviously, to memorize a few pieces at a time. That means spacing your cram times well so that you can break down your work into small chunks and push it into the long term, bit by bit.

We also have a hard time memorizing material we don't understand. See which of these lists you can memorize faster:

sad	das
and	nda
pat	tpa
put	utp
yes	eys

The nonsense syllables are much harder. Keep this in mind the next time you consider cramming for an exam without understanding the content clearly.

Still, even when the content is clear, memorization takes much more effort than simple reading, and it can be difficult. To do it at all, you first must want to do it. That doesn't mean you'll *enjoy* the work; for this task "want" means simply that you have the determination to get it done well enough to succeed on the exam. If your mother makes you go to the store for four items, you'll probably forget at least one, since you didn't want to do it. If she bets you a dollar that you won't remember, you're more likely to get everything. You still won't enjoy the trip, but you have an incentive to lock the list into your mind.

An understanding of the material and an incentive for remembering it are two important factors in memorization—

and luckily, there are many tricks and techniques that make the effort easier. The ones that will work best for you are those that best fit your learning style. If you are a visual person, write or draw your material, and force yourself to "see it" with your mind's eye. If your ears are your keenest tools, read everything aloud or listen to your own tape recordings of it. If you need to use your entire body, try dancing, tapping your fingers, or other physical techniques.

Experiment with some of these techniques and see which are the most effective for you:

- One way to lock something into your memory is to look at it hard, read it out loud, then close your eyes and say it aloud again. Make yourself "hear" and "see" it mentally. Finally, try to force those words and images into the "back of your brain." If you do it right, you can almost feel the items being "lodged" in your head as they move from your short-term into your long-term memory.

- Another technique you might find helpful is to make mental pictures of the material's content. Are you studying about the French Revolution? Then paint a picture in your mind's eye of all that happened on, say, Bastille Day. Then, to recall facts about it, you can "look" at that mental picture for reminders. Or make a mental picture of important pages in your textbooks. You may find that you can actually "read" those pages while you are taking the test.

- Some people find absurdity useful as a memory aid. Suppose, for instance, that you had to memorize this passage:

"To compare means to find resemblances and differences between qualities and characteristics of two or more items, stressing similarities. To criticize means to express your judgment in evaluating the worth, accuracy, or significance of the topic presented."

You might better remember "compare" by forming a mental image of two animals that are part cat and part dog. And perhaps to remember "criticize" you can imagine yourself as a clown in a circus giving horntoots to express your judgments.

• You can also try breaking your material down into smaller chunks or reorganizing it. To memorize all those definitions on pages 71–77, for instance, work on the "a" word first, then on all the words beginning with "c" next, then "d," and so forth. Tick off on your fingers how many "a's," "c's," "d's," etc., you need to recall so that you keep better track of them.

• Grouping items helps, too. If you have to know the capitals of all fifty states, for instance, group them by geographical regions—"New England," "Northwest," and so on. Then, you'll have about eight clumps to memorize rather than fifty unrelated names.

• When you need to remember large volumes of information, find key words in each paragraph or section. Memorize those, and use them to stimulate your recollection of the whole mass.

In addition to these techniques, there are many useful memory tricks that will not only ease and lock materials into your mind but also act as hooks to bring it out when needed. For instance:

• Initial words or *acronyms*. The initials of the Great Lakes spell HOMES: *H*uron, *O*ntario, *M*ichigan, *E*rie, and *S*upe-

Bigger Deals

rior. *M*y *D*ear *A*unt *S*ally is a reminder that in math, *M*ultiplication and *D*ivision are done before *A*ddition and *S*ubtraction. The first letter of each of the short words on page 88 spell "sappy," and rearranging the order of the nonsense syllables so you can think about them as "tuned" might make them possible to remember.

- Rhymes. "The defeat of the Moors at the Battle of Tours."
  "In 1492 Columbus sailed the ocean blue."
  "I before E except after C, or when sounded as A as in neighbor or weigh."
- Rhythm and melody. Set the words to music or a beat, and the jingle will be easy to remember, even when you're dealing with complex mathematical or scientific formulas.

When you apply tricks and techniques such as these to your style and your material, you'll find that your rhymes and jingles will be easy to remember and will trigger your memory of the actual material.

However you go about it, when you've memorized a chunk of material, write it out and/or talk it into a tape recorder, referring to your notes as little as possible. You will know that you've got it down pat when you can recite it accurately without physically seeing or hearing it.

TAKE A DEEP BREATH!

And now, there's only one more preparation step to take before the exam—relax!

The tension-relieving techniques described in Chapter 4 will help ease tensions while you're studying, let you get to sleep the night before the exam, and relax you during even the biggest of big tests. Why not try some of them now? They're simple but surprisingly effective.

The study skills and test-taking techniques that you've been learning in these chapters are effective, too. They may seem like a big effort at first, but you'll soon find that they're more than worth the trouble.

You are as ready as you will ever be or can be, and now you need to concentrate your energy and attention on the test itself.

JUST IN CASE

To be honest, of course, all that relaxation and positive thinking may not do you much good if that universally feared student's nightmare comes true and, for whatever reason, you simply do not know the answers to the questions you confront on a test. Readying yourself for action in that sort of situation should also be a part of your psychological preparation for exam taking. So, just in case, keep this advice in mind: *Don't ever simply walk away from a test!*

One way or another, you can always salvage something from even the most incomprehensible exam, if you stick it out and follow through, so you needn't consider this situation a nightmare.

Here are some examples:

At one university that, like many others, gives course credit to students who score well enough on an exam in a given subject even though they have not taken the course itself, enrollees studied chemistry on their own all summer in order to pass the equivalency exam. About 300 students took their seats in the testing room. Within 15 minutes after the test papers were distributed, about 150 walked out, because the questions were so much harder than what they had expected and what they could handle. Of the 150 left, perhaps 50 actually knew how to answer the questions with some degree of accuracy. The rest simply marked down something and later laughed about the foolishness of their efforts.

Yet, when the scores came out a week later, almost all of those 100 "chemistry dummies" found that they had received credit for at least one semester of the course. Why? Perhaps the professors purposely had designed a difficult test. Or perhaps they realized that the test was more difficult than they had planned, and so graded leniently or marked papers on a gentle curve, so that the "walk-outs" gave the "stayers" a half-decent score.

A junior high student, facing an exam whose content surprised him, made a few notes for each question, then explained at the bottom of his test paper that, although he had studied, he didn't seem to be able to understand the material, and he asked for extra help. He did not fail the exam.

Through her own fault, a high school girl had not been able to study for a test given by a teacher she really respected. Rather than skip class or leave the room early, she wrote on her paper: "I'm sorry that I didn't study. I hope that I'll do better on the next one, because I really enjoy this class." The teacher allowed her to make up the test a few weeks later.

The moral of these stories: Don't ever just walk out of a test or turn in a totally blank paper (or worse, a paper with a rude comment on it). You might know more than you thought you did; or your scratchy notes just might be better than the answers of enough of your classmates to get you a passing grade.

Most teachers, like the rest of us, are willing to give help when it is needed, and most respect honesty. So even when you feel panicky, there's no call for panic: you always have positive options.

MEETING THE TEST

But you do know how to approach that test, don't you? No matter how big or important the exam is, you will follow the same steps described in Chapter 2:

preview: look the whole test over first, and allot your time
view: go through the test methodically, doing the easiest parts first
review: go back over your answers and check for accuracy

That same procedure applies to the tests that make everyone the most nervous: standardized examinations.

7. Taking the Mystery Out of Standardized Tests:

WHAT THEY ARE AND WHY

Four-year-olds take standardized aptitude tests to get into high-power nursery schools. First-graders take standardized achievement tests to get them in practice for the "real thing" in second grade. By the time students hit the first year of senior high school, they are probably all too familiar with those booklets printed with little blank boxes. People continue to face them throughout college and graduate school—and beyond, when they apply for jobs or join the military. These are the tests that still frighten everyone—students, parents, and teachers—the most, in part because they seem powerful and mysterious in themselves. To make them easier to deal with, let's first clear away some of the mystery and myth.

The very name and form of these tests somehow make them seem perfect and all-important. Yet the adjective "standardized" has a very specific meaning. A test is "standardized" when the same questions, the same instructions, the same time limits, and the same scoring system are applied to every person taking it. Also, it grades test takers by measuring each one of them against a *standard* set of skills, responses, or levels of age or achievement.

WHY WERE THOSE TESTS EVER INVENTED?
There was a time when the belief in the power and perfection of these tests was much more widespread than, luckily, it is today; and it can help to keep them in perspective if you understand some of their background.

When our great-grandparents and great-greats were kids, back as recently as the end of the last century, there was no need for standardized tests. Kids growing up in many places then didn't *have* to go to school, and if they did, they weren't required to stay long—and often family finances made it necessary for them to go to work at early ages. At that time, teachers' grade books had plenty of space to record the "achievements" of those who went to school; since relatively few young people went on to college, the admissions process was a highly personal affair.

But around the turn of the century, some major events occurred. The economy changed and grew, making it possible for children to attend school rather than work to bring in extra income. More and more communities made education compulsory. And, with government help, new colleges and universities began opening across the continent. The result: too many student achievements for space in grade books, and too many college applicants for "the personal approach."

Fortunately for educators, while all this growth was going

on, development of a new tool—"mental measurement"—was in progress. In Europe in the late 1800's, researchers in the new science of psychology had decided that it was possible to measure a person's intelligence and personality by means of relatively simple tests.

During the first decade of the twentieth century, means of standardizing these tests—of making the same measurement valid and reliable for administration to a great number of people—were devised. (A test is considered *valid* if investigation proves that it actually measures what it is intended to measure. It is called *reliable* if statistics show that it does that measuring accurately and consistently in most cases most of the time.)

The U.S. Army made the first broad-scale use of such tests to classify recruits during World War I, and soon state education departments and private organizations were developing examinations to test entire school populations.

Since such tests were so convenient and so necessary, wouldn't it be tempting to believe that they were "the perfect solution"? Certainly—and unfortunately that's what happened, at least for a time. The tests were born during an era of absolute faith in science; and it came to be assumed that aptitude, ability, intelligence, and personality could be measured as accurately as, say, chemical ingredients in a gas. There was little or no consideration given to the fact that people come in infinite varieties and from different backgrounds. Too often, people—parents, teachers, guidance counselors, college administrators, even students—came to make vitally important judgments solely on the basis of a young person's test scores; and to make sure students did well on them, teachers often taught only what the tests would ask, rather than work to convey knowledge for its own sake.

Because of such misuse of and overreliance on the tests, in the 1970's various groups began to challenge their validity and to question the methods of their construction.

Test takers have benefited from the resulting controversy in several ways:

The test makers appear to have worked hard to revise their batteries toward making them bias free and better geared to testing what the majority of schools teach. Most provide detailed instructions on both the purposes of each test and the methods of sharing their results with parents and students for effective guidance.

Also, many schools no longer require "intelligence tests" that perhaps unfairly pigeonhole people at an early age as "dumb."

Laws requiring testing organizations to remove the secrecy from their methods and allowing challenges to their scoring should make standardized exams fairer and more accurate.

An understanding of the true nature of all forms of such tests has already helped put them in the right perspective: By and large they are valid and reliable measures of a person's aptitude, learning, personality and even, perhaps, intelligence. However, they are not absolute, and those who make important decisions about other people's lives now know better than to rely solely on test scores, especially because the tests have been shown to be *not* perfect.

Parents who suffered through standardized tests years ago and were taught the myths about them may tell their children: "They're all that counts," "Once your score is in, it can't be changed," and "You can*not* study for them!" But none of these statements is true, and today's student should maintain a healthy attitude toward them. Yes, they are important, and you should take them seriously. No, they are not tablets of absolute truth and wisdom, so you should view them realistically.

WHAT YOU'RE UP AGAINST: DIFFERENT TYPES OF STANDARDIZED TESTS

In order to be realistic about standardized tests, you also need to know as much detail about them as possible. First, though all of them may look alike, with their little answer boxes and their boldface sections of instructions, they are not. Different tests have different purposes. Some are designed to rate achievement, some to measure aptitude, others to probe intelligence or personality. The chart on pages 138-151 describes the major standardized tests of all types.

Among *achievement tests,* you must take any of those that your state, county, or city requires of all students in public, private, or parochial schools in order to assess the quality of your education at different stages. Also, if you apply to a special public school, to a private school, or to many colleges, you will probably be required to take other achievement tests. (Students for whom English is a second language, or others with special educational needs or interests, will likely encounter additional special achievement tests.) No matter what the main purpose of each achievement test given during your schooling, your scores will become a part of your permanent record, and will play an important part in your class placement, the guidance you receive, and, often, your teachers' impressions of you.

One achievement test that has an even more direct effect on students is the "minimum competency" exam required by many school systems. Given in the senior year of high school or beginning in junior high and repeated till senior year, these tests are used to make sure that, before young people leave high school for the wider world, they can read, write, and compute well enough to make their way—to read a want ad, for instance, fill out a job application, or manage basic banking.

You will take *aptitude tests* if you apply to any sort of special school, to almost any college in the country, or for many jobs you might seek. Also, some school systems include aptitude tests as a required part of their program. *Aptitude* means natural ability or talent. In theory, aptitude tests measure students' inborn tendencies toward a specific skill or expertise—whether academics, music, hairdressing, law, acting, fashion, or the like. In the early 1980's, testing critics pointed out that many of the standardized aptitude tests were in fact achievement tests, because test items assumed that the test taker had a certain degree of learning or knowledge. Whatever the facts, if you take these tests while you are in school, your scores become a part of your permanent record. They also will influence your educational path, directly and indirectly. For example, you will not be able to enter music (or whatever) school if you don't test well on the music aptitude test. Indirectly, your scores will influence your teachers' views of you. They may place different expectations on you if, for instance, you test high in verbal "aptitude" but do poorly in English.

Standardized tests designed to measure *intelligence,* especially those administered to large groups, have also been widely criticized in recent years as being achievement tests. Critics say that the test makers tend to be middle-class, white, suburban males who create, perhaps naturally, questions based on their own backgrounds and thus assume a type of information that only people like themselves have absorbed. This criticism came as the result of a questioning of what intelligence really is and whether it can be measured by any exam. For these and other reasons, many schools and school systems no longer require "intelligence" testing, and you may encounter such tests only if you or your parents choose to have you take them.

Personality or *psychological* tests are validated against a profile created by the answers of many others who have been identified specifically as being one type of personality or another. For instance, someone whose answers closely match answers given by an "authoritarian" type of person would be considered "authoritarian." You may not have to take them unless you choose to, or unless you apply for a job or enter a school that requires them. Many schools, colleges, and employers do make use of such tests; or at some point in your life you may decide to take them on your own, because, when properly used, they can be quite helpful in providing guidance.

WHAT THESE TESTS ARE TESTING

Your first step in coping with *any* standardized test is to ask for some basic information: What is the purpose of this test? What is it supposed to measure? Why are we taking it now? When such questions are asked in a manner that shows you are seeking information and not posing a challenge, teachers and test administrators should be happy to give you good explanations, because this will help shape your attitude and approach to a particular test.

You should also learn details about what the test scorers are looking for. For instance, is this test, or a portion of it, a "speed test" or a "power test"? A speed test gives you credit for the number of items you complete within the time allowed; a power test looks more to the quality of your answers, especially to those questions considered to be more difficult.

How much of the exam will consist of "recognition" items—multiple choice, true-false or other short answers—and how much will be *free response*—essay questions or others in which you must come up with the answers yourself?

Will this exam test *maximum* performance or *typical* performance? On an achievement test, you will want to perform at your maximum ability to show yourself at your best. On a personality-type battery you want your responses to be a typical representation of you.

Some standardized tests, or portions of them, are more interested in the process you used to arrive at your answer than in the answer itself that you produced. Having information on the *process* versus *product* aspect of a test will also guide you effectively.

There is no reason why the construction of standardized tests should be a mystery, since their purpose is to discover what you know or who you are—not to trip you up on a technicality.

HOW YOU GET WHAT YOU GET

There is also no reason why your scores should be a mystery, and understanding the methods of scoring such exams is not difficult. You know that if you miss one out of ten on a classroom true-false test, you get a 90. You know that if, on a bigger class exam, you miss only one question, but it carries a weight of 25 points, you get a 75. You have learned by now that, depending on the teacher or the class, both your 90 and your 75 might be a B, because in one instance you might be graded in absolute terms and in the other your grade might reflect a comparison with the scores the rest of your class got on the same test.

Standardized tests are scored in similar ways, but the system is a bit more complex.

First, your responses are compared against a standard answer key. In many large-scale tests, computers grade short-answer questions electronically. Any essay questions are read and compared against ideal responses. For psychological or personality inventories, testers have a set of answers given by various groups of test takers whose personality profiles are known: for instance, "Schizophrenics tend to answer these questions in this way...." or "People with an aptitude for forestry usually respond in such a way to these questions...."

Each score is assigned a number, in some cases after a value is deducted for wrong answers. That number is your *raw score,* just like that 90 or 75 on your quiz or exam.

Then, that raw score is converted according to a *scale* that takes into account varying difficulty of questions and varying weight that the testers feel should be assigned to different sections of the exam. (In the same way, missing one short-answer question on an exam may cost you two points; missing a big question on the same test can cost you twenty-five.)

Finally, your scale is compared to those of all others who

have taken the same test. Using statistical techniques that mathematically take into account the possibility for technical errors, scorers come up with your *percentile* score. If 98% of the test takers did worse than you on a section of the test, for instance, your percentile score is 98. If 50% did worse than you, you have a score of 50%. In the same way, your classroom teacher may compare your work on the test with that of others in your class and decide that your 75 is worth a B; since most people didn't do too well, you got a better letter grade than a 75 would indicate or than you would have received if your classmates had all done better. Some test makers also group your percentiles into broader chunks, such as *quartiles* by dividing the percentile ranges into fourths, or into *stanines* by dividing the percentile ranges into ninths. With an 82%, for instance, you would be in the fourth quartile (or top quarter) of testers, or in the eighth stanine (or next-to-best ninth) among the nationwide group of test takers.

In one area, standardized scoring is quite different from classroom grading. In each exam, makers of mass tests include experimental questions. Although these questions appear to be part of the test as a whole, your responses to them will not be part of your final score but will indicate whether the questions should be included on future tests. Psychological inventories also include what is called a "lie scale:" questions whose responses indicate to evaluators that the test taker was not being completely honest and open on the exam as a whole.

When you receive the grades for any standardized tests you take, your teacher, guidance counselor, or whoever administered the test should go over your score with you. Even though the scoring system is in fact not too mysterious, the numbers, symbols, and tables that confront you can seem confusing. In case no one volunteers to explain your test results, you should ask.

8. Preparing for Standardized Tests:

YOU *CAN* COACH YOURSELF

Much of the myth, mystery, and confusion that has grown up over the years around standardized tests has concerned whether or not you could—or even should—study for them. On the one hand, major test makers maintained that studying for any but achievement tests in specific topics was unnecessary and futile. On the other hand, it was not uncommon for entire school systems to build their courses of study around preparation for a standardized test. Some families spent large sums on tutoring courses for their children, while countless other kids went into the tests completely cold.

Now it is generally agreed that there are many ways in which to prepare for all standardized tests without having teachers waste educational time in teaching only "to the tests" (though most teachers will try to be sure that they cover what school-administered exams will test).

WHERE TO START

Here are some general guidelines for preparation:

- You will test better if you study well. Once you form the habit of studying according to the techniques outlined in Chapter 3—of organizing your material into a format comfortable for you, for instance, and of reviewing regularly and constantly—you will absorb and retain more information than you realize, and much more than you could by cramming it in. No one, not even the coach in a "cram school," pretends that you can improve test scores by last-minute cramming.

  If, however, you begin a few months ahead of a standardized test to spend a little time each day working with the type of material you are likely to encounter on the test, you will be warmed up and ready, like an athlete who spends several months warming up for a big event. If you are weak in a certain area you'll be tested on, spend extra time trying to get that subject under your belt.

- By and large, no matter what the subject, standardized tests require problem solving, with either words or numbers. Exercise your problem-solving ability. Using items from sample tests or review books, practice thinking through each problem or question. Don't give up too fast and check the answers in the back, since you won't be able to do that on the real test. Work the problems through out loud or with paper and pencil, if necessary. If the answer still doesn't come, tuck it into the back of your mind and move on to the others, then return and begin again. When you score your practice tests, read or figure out how each right answer was arrived at, especially for any questions that you missed, and use those techniques the next time you practice.

- Boost your vocabulary. For almost every section of every standardized test (even those that say they are testing nonverbal skills), you need a good, solid grasp of English and the meaning of words in order to do well. You will not need to memorize the unabridged dictionary to accomplish this. But, especially if you've never been much of a reader, you should devote time and effort to become thoroughly familiar with common prefixes, suffixes, and the roots of words. In this way, you can make a well-educated guess when you confront a word with which you are totally unfamiliar. The books listed on pages 154–155 will help.
- Increase your speed and familiarity with numbers. You'll be asked to make a lot of computations quickly, so even if you're a math whiz, make sure you're well practiced in basic arithmetic skills. Spend some extra time each day working the unassigned problems in your math book, especially the review sections that go over past material. Concentrate on working as quickly as possible, and if some types of problems cause you extra trouble, focus your efforts on becoming comfortable with them.
- Coaching can be effective for all types of standardized tests, primarily because of the practice it offers. Your school may run practice sessions prior to the PSAT or the SAT. If it doesn't, see if you can organize one under the leadership of a teacher or counselor who is willing to give the time. (Remember, your school wants you to do well on these "biggies," if only because it makes the school look good!) At least get together with one or more friends for your own practice

Preparing for Standardized Tests

sessions. If possible, round up a student who has already taken the test, for advice from the horse's mouth. If you do want to seek more "professional" assistance, see the advice on pages 159–160.

- For your review or self-coaching, make *full* use of sample tests and other material available from the testing companies. Several good review books and study guides are also available (see pages 152–154). The more familiar you are with the actual test formats, the better you will do. Not only will you pick up specific skills, but you will have the secure feeling of knowing exactly what you are facing. The best way to prepare is to practice, practice, practice!

TESTING FORMATS

The content that you can expect to face when you are allowed to open the test booklet will, of course, vary.

Achievement tests for specific knowledge areas will contain direct requests for facts or skills related to that area. Foreign-language exams, for instance, will include vocabulary, translation, and reading comprehension; and advanced math and science tests contain both problems to solve and theorems to interpret.

Aptitude test content depends on the aptitude to be tested—law-school entrance exams will contain different material from those for medical-school or high-school entrance. In general, however, aptitude tests go about testing skills and abilities by using these types of questions or problems:

Verbal relationships—synonyms, antonyms, word analogies, and sentence completion to test reasoning ability.

Comprehension skills—reading passages on which a number of content questions are asked.

Language ability—sentences, paragraphs, punctuation, and spelling to correct.

Listening—spoken problems or passages to test your skill at understanding what goes on in a classroom.

Mathematical abilities—items involving actual computation in arithmetic, algebra, and geometry, and those testing your grasp of spatial and quantitative relationships and concepts in order to judge your reasoning ability.

Writing ability—some aptitude and achievement tests require the writing of at least one passage on an assigned topic, while others include long passages to edit and reorganize.

You will find brief sample questions from each type of exam later in this chapter, on pages 117–123; but you can get full-fledged samples in the books listed on pages 154–155 or by writing to the companies and organizations that design the test. (Some samples are free; others cost nominal amounts.) Their addresses are listed on pages 156–158, and they are quite willing to send test takers information, including basic review outlines that tell what you need to know, and sample tests. A list of groups and agencies that can provide help and information on various aspects of studying and testing appears on pages 158–159.

TECHNICALITIES

Some practical matters are important to consider as part of

Preparing for Standardized Tests

your test preparation. If they sound silly, remember that the "little things" can trip you up just as badly as the big mistakes!

- Find out well in advance what test you will be taking: there's little point in reviewing for the wrong one.
- Be sure you have to take the test. Everyone must take the ones required by their school systems. Some schools or colleges require one form of admissions test; others, another; and some, none at all.

If you are taking a test that is not given by your school for its own purposes, you will probably have to register for it well in advance and pay a small fee. Be sure you do so in time, or you will not be able to take the exam. Your school will provide instructions on how to go about this process, but it is up to you to pay attention and follow through.

- Find out where and when the test will be given. Mark the date on your calendar and arrange in advance to get there in plenty of time. If you arrive late, you may not be allowed to take the test—and at best you will cheat yourself by having to rush through it. If you must miss a test-administration day at school, arrange for a makeup right away.
- As T day approaches, take good care of yourself! Eat right, get enough exercise, and sleep as much as possible. Get an especially good rest the night before the test, but be sure to set your alarm in plenty of time to have a good breakfast and be on time.
- Dress comfortably, and take with you to the exam site pencils, gum, candy, tissues, a watch, your reading glasses—anything you might need to keep yourself at ease during the test, including a snack or lunch if you're going to need it. Ask

if you will need a special type of pencil or pen, or if you will have to show I.D.

- Do *not* take any books, notes, or disallowed items such as calculators. Even if you have no intention of using them, you might make the test administrators suspicious. You do not want to do *anything* that will even seem like possible cheating, because cheaters' scores are disqualified.

In taking standardized tests, handling the nitty-gritty details can be as important as grasping the content of the exam.

IN THE TESTING ROOM

Part of the nitty-gritty of doing well on these exams has to do with what you can expect when you walk into the testing room.

"I was really prepared for the test," said one young woman who had taken the PSAT very seriously, "until I walked into the room and saw all those chairs and strange faces—then I got nervous!"

We talked earlier about studying and practicing in an environment that says "Test!" A typing student who could do close to 90 words a minute (and that's a lot) was totally paralyzed by the noise of 120 other typists hitting the keys.

If you are taking a standardized test such as the PSAT, the SAT, the SSAT, or others that are not required by the school you currently attend, you can expect to enter a large, bright room and be seated at a desk or desk-chair well separated from your neighboring test taker, who is likely to be a stranger. Supervisors—or "proctors" or "monitors" (about one for every 30 test takers) will be on hand to police the test.

Their job is not only to patrol a certain section of the room to guard against cheating, but to make sure that every person in their sector is comfortable and having no personal problem that needs attention. But they will be *walking,* and you must try to ignore them unless you need them (you will need their permission to leave the room, for instance).

Even if you are taking "simply" a school-required test, you should have the same expectation about the testing site. You need not expect to see total strangers in the room, but you probably will see teachers who are not regularly in your classroom, since most schools assign alternate teachers to monitor tests.

So, you're in a strange room, or a room with strangers, and you're all hyped up for "The Test." The first thing you're asked to fill out has nothing to do with analogies or formulas, but with a question like "What was your mother's maiden name?" Detailed personal questionnaires precede most standardized tests. They serve two purposes: They make sure that the test taker is really who he or she claims to be. (Wouldn't it be great to have your genius cousin take your exam!) They also provide the test publishers and the educational system with a mass of statistics about the country's school population, so that administrators and the public can keep tabs on long-term trends. If nationwide scores show that rural tenth-graders are doing poorly in science, for instance, school systems can respond, but only if the personal-information forms pinpoint the facts. Also, the preliminaries aid in your individual guidance, so they're important; and while you're dealing with them, you'll probably find that you're also getting geared up to work with the "real stuff."

DEALING WITH DIRECTIONS

Once everyone has finished filling out the questionnaires, you'll be told how to proceed with the test. The directions for proceeding will, of course, vary with each type of test, but you can expect to see a set of instructions that will cover the following points:

- An introduction to the overall exam: how many sections it contains, what they are, how much time is allotted to each one, and whether or not you can work on more than one section at once (in most cases, this is *not* permitted).
- Step-by-step procedures for answering the questions: how you go about deciding on an answer, and how you mark your choice—whether to write in the question booklet or on a separate answer sheet, to use a pencil (your own or a special one) or pen, whether you can "scratch" on the booklet or a separate paper.
- Suggestions on how to go about working the test: The SAT, for instance, advises not wasting time over questions that seem too difficult, but to work as quickly and accurately as possible. It explains that wrong answers lose you points, and recommends not making any other than well-educated guesses. On the other hand, the American College Testing program (ACT) says that you will not be penalized for guessing and so should answer every question.
- Each section of the test will have its own set of instructions, but you will not be able to read those until the supervisor tells you that you may.
- For some standardized tests, you will hear, rather than read, the instructions. All of them provide some spoken directions (such as what to do if you have a problem or a ques-

tion, and when to begin and end). These are standardized, too, so that every test supervisor around the country is reading exactly the same thing.

TAKING THE TEST

Okay, you know what to do, your pencil is poised, you've taken a deep breath to relax, and you're about to begin. Now what?

• Remember that your time allotment, your accuracy, and your attention to detail are more important for these exams, which will be scored by anonymous stencils or machines, than for a classroom test graded by a familiar teacher, so listen to the test administrator's instructions and read the written directions especially carefully. If you have any questions, ask them!

• Do not make any mark on the test paper other than your intended answer. On tests that are scored electronically, you risk confusing your score if you make marks on anything but whatever scratch paper is provided; and on hand-scored exams, the grader may not know which mark you meant. When you have made a mistake, or change your mind, erase completely. On multiple-choice questions, mark only one box—otherwise, the answer will count as wrong.

• Keep your question book and any separate answer sheet close to each other so that reading and marking are both convenient. And be sure to fill in the proper row! If your answers are right but accidentally marked in the wrong row, you may fail the entire test.

You will be better able to cope with any standardized tests

when you realize that they are little different from any of the other tests you take week in and week out. So handle them by the same procedure: preview, view, and review.

- Quickly read through the entire section you will be working on. Roughly allocate your time, and answer first the questions that are easiest. Rather than waste time chewing over one you're unsure of, mark the ones you know. However, avoid picking the most obvious answer automatically: Most items have two choices that "look good," but only one that is right.

- Then go back and work on the harder ones. Even if you are working on a test that penalizes you for guessing, you have several methods available within the test itself to make a well-educated guess, so don't panic or despair. Make sure that you have read the question accurately. Eliminate choices that you know are impossible. Look for clues within the question or problem itself. Try rewording the question or reformulating the problem in a way that makes sense to you. Compare it with similar questions or problems that you were able to answer. If you're torn between two answers, go with the one that you think the testers are more likely to be looking for—the more general one, for instance. If you truly think that the question contains an ambiguity that makes more than one answer seem correct, raise your hand and ask about it.

- When the time you set aside for rechecking comes, go back and recheck! Review your answers and make sure you've marked the boxes accurately. Erase all errors *fully*. Even if you are allowed to leave the testing room whenever you are ready, use all of your time. Wise test takers know that there is always something more they can do on an exam.

WHAT TO EXPECT

Here's a sample of some types of questions you are likely to encounter on some of the most widely administered standardized tests. These are not, needless to say, actual test questions now in use; rather, they are examples provided by the test publishers to help students become familiar with the exams.

These are sample test questions from the DAT:

......is to water as eat is to......

A continue——drive
B foot——enemy
C drink——food
D girl——industry
E drink——enemy

......is to night as breakfast is to......

A supper——corner
B gentle——morning
C door——corner
D flow——enjoy
E supper——morning

......is to one as second is to......

A two——middle
B first——fire
C queen——hill
D first——two
E rain——fire

Examples reproduced by permission from the Differential Aptitude Tests. Copyright © 1982, 1980, 1974, 1973 by The Psychological Corporation. All rights reserved.

The following are sample test questions from the ACT Assessment Mathematical Usage Test:

What is the average (arithmetic mean) of the set of numbers shown below?

$$\{6, 12, 13, 8, 7, 7, 10\}$$

A. 7
B. 9
C. 10½
D. 31½
E. 63

If $\dfrac{0}{a} + \dfrac{3}{b} = 1$, then $b = ?$

F. 0
G. ⅓
H. 1
J. 3
K. 4

A salesperson is paid $100 per week plus 7% of the amount of her sales, s. Which equation could be used to find her weekly pay, p, in dollars?

F. $p = (1.07)^s$
G. $p = 1.07s$
H. $p = 100s + .07s$
J. $p = .07(100 + s)$
K. $p = 100 + .07s$

Copyright 1982 by The American College Testing Program. All rights reserved. Reproduced with permission.

Here are some sample questions from the ACT Assessment Social Studies Reading Test:

Which individual could be accurately described as a *white collar criminal?*
F. A prisoner who has been assigned prison clerical duties
G. A middle-class clothing store clerk who joins a heroin-smuggling ring
H. The director of a crime syndicate
J. An administrative or professional person who uses his position for illegal gain

Which of the following statements would a social scientist consider to be a statement of fact?
A. Juvenile delinquency is a growing curse on society.
B. We will have a happier nation if the number of divorces does not surpass the number of marriages.
C. The total population of the U.S. is increasing each year.
D. Congress should pass a law reducing the number of immigrants admitted each year.

Which term indicates a market system in which there is only one possible seller?
A. Oligopoly
B. Oligopsony
C. Monopsony
D. Monopoly

Copyright 1982 by The American College Testing Program. All rights reserved. Reproduced with permission.

Here are some sample test questions from the SRA Achievement Series, Level H:

Reading Comprehension. This is a test of how well you understand what you read. Read the passage and then answer the sample question that follows it.

Most people seldom think of the great ocean of air that surrounds the earth. They breathe in oxygen and breathe out carbon dioxide. They enjoy the sunshine or come out of the rain without thinking of the great forces that play upon the earth.

The atmosphere has many layers, each with its own characteristics. The layer closest to the earth is called the troposphere. This layer extends from the earth's surface to a height that varies from five miles at the poles to eleven miles at the equator. It is in this part of the atmosphere that the forms of weather generally experienced on earth occur.

There is no rain, snow, or sleet, no weather fronts, tornadoes, thunder, or lightning above the troposphere. In fact, only a few kinds of clouds are found above it. The temperature decreases with height in this layer of the atmosphere, ranging to as low as $-80°C$ over the equator.

The main purpose of this passage is to

A. show how important the atmosphere is to human beings

B. give general information about the atmosphere

C. describe how the troposphere effects the amount of rainfall

D. provide information about air pollution

Reference Materials. This is a test of how well you can find and use information.

Preparing for Standardized Tests

Use the dictionary page below to answer the question that follows it.

DICTIONARY PAGE

mac ad am (mə kad′ əm) *n* **1.** a road made of crushed stones held together by tar or asphalt

mar tyr (märt′ ər) *n* **1.** a person put to death for refusing to give up religious beliefs **2.** a person who willingly sacrifices life or something else of importance for a principle **3.** a constant sufferer **4.** someone who apparently enjoys suffering

mas quer ade (mas′ kə rād′) *n* **1.** a costume party **2.** a costume to wear to such a party **3.** the pretense of having or owning something that is valued **4.** deceiving by being showy

mech a nism (mek′ ə niz əm) *n* **1.** a piece of machinery **2.** an operation done by a machine

mez za nine (mez′ ən ēn) *n* **1.** a floor between two main floors in a building **2.** a floor that sticks out like a balcony **3.** the lowest balcony in a theater **4.** the first few rows of seats in the lowest balcony

mis place (mis plās′) *v* **1.** to forget where something has been placed **2.** to put in the wrong place

Which meaning of the word <u>masquerade</u> applies to the following sentence? <u>Ramona's masquerade consisted of glasses, a wig, and a baggy dress.</u>

A. Definition 1
B. Definition 2
C. Definition 3
D. Definition 4

From *A Message to Students: About the SRA Achievement Series.* Copyright © Science Research Associates, Inc., 1981. Reproduced with permission.

These are portions of the ACT Assessment answer sheet:

If the information on your test center admission ticket is complete and correct, put down your pencil and wait for further instructions.

If any corrections are necessary, complete ONLY those blocks below for which the information on your test center admission ticket is INCOMPLETE or INCORRECT. Leave the other blocks blank.

F — **NAME CORRECTION**

Last Name | First Name | MI

© 1982 by The American College Testing Program. All rights reserved. Reproduced with permission.

TEST 1: English Usage

1 Ⓐ Ⓑ Ⓒ Ⓓ	10 Ⓕ Ⓖ Ⓗ Ⓘ	19 Ⓐ Ⓑ Ⓒ Ⓓ	28 Ⓕ Ⓖ Ⓗ Ⓘ
2 Ⓕ Ⓖ Ⓗ Ⓘ	11 Ⓐ Ⓑ Ⓒ Ⓓ	20 Ⓕ Ⓖ Ⓗ Ⓘ	29 Ⓐ Ⓑ Ⓒ Ⓓ
3 Ⓐ Ⓑ Ⓒ Ⓓ	12 Ⓕ Ⓖ Ⓗ Ⓘ	21 Ⓐ Ⓑ Ⓒ Ⓓ	30 Ⓕ Ⓖ Ⓗ Ⓘ
4 Ⓕ Ⓖ Ⓗ Ⓘ	13 Ⓐ Ⓑ Ⓒ Ⓓ	22 Ⓕ Ⓖ Ⓗ Ⓘ	31 Ⓐ Ⓑ Ⓒ Ⓓ
5 Ⓐ Ⓑ Ⓒ Ⓓ	14 Ⓕ Ⓖ Ⓗ Ⓘ	23 Ⓐ Ⓑ Ⓒ Ⓓ	32 Ⓕ Ⓖ Ⓗ Ⓘ
6 Ⓕ Ⓖ Ⓗ Ⓘ	15 Ⓐ Ⓑ Ⓒ Ⓓ	24 Ⓕ Ⓖ Ⓗ Ⓘ	33 Ⓐ Ⓑ Ⓒ Ⓓ
7 Ⓐ Ⓑ Ⓒ Ⓓ	16 Ⓕ Ⓖ Ⓗ Ⓘ	25 Ⓐ Ⓑ Ⓒ Ⓓ	34 Ⓕ Ⓖ Ⓗ Ⓘ
8 Ⓕ Ⓖ Ⓗ Ⓘ	17 Ⓐ Ⓑ Ⓒ Ⓓ	26 Ⓕ Ⓖ Ⓗ Ⓘ	35 Ⓐ Ⓑ Ⓒ Ⓓ
9 Ⓐ Ⓑ Ⓒ Ⓓ	18 Ⓕ Ⓖ Ⓗ Ⓘ	27 Ⓐ Ⓑ Ⓒ Ⓓ	36 Ⓕ Ⓖ Ⓗ Ⓘ

TEST 2: Mathematics Usage

1 Ⓐ Ⓑ Ⓒ Ⓓ Ⓔ	6 Ⓕ Ⓖ Ⓗ Ⓙ Ⓚ	11 Ⓐ Ⓑ Ⓒ Ⓓ Ⓔ	16 Ⓕ Ⓖ Ⓗ Ⓙ Ⓚ
2 Ⓕ Ⓖ Ⓗ Ⓙ Ⓚ	7 Ⓐ Ⓑ Ⓒ Ⓓ Ⓔ	12 Ⓕ Ⓖ Ⓗ Ⓙ Ⓚ	17 Ⓐ Ⓑ Ⓒ Ⓓ Ⓔ
3 Ⓐ Ⓑ Ⓒ Ⓓ Ⓔ	8 Ⓕ Ⓖ Ⓗ Ⓙ Ⓚ	13 Ⓐ Ⓑ Ⓒ Ⓓ Ⓔ	18 Ⓕ Ⓖ Ⓗ Ⓙ Ⓚ
4 Ⓕ Ⓖ Ⓗ Ⓙ Ⓚ	9 Ⓐ Ⓑ Ⓒ Ⓓ Ⓔ	14 Ⓕ Ⓖ Ⓗ Ⓙ Ⓚ	19 Ⓐ Ⓑ Ⓒ Ⓓ Ⓔ
5 Ⓐ Ⓑ Ⓒ Ⓓ Ⓔ	10 Ⓕ Ⓖ Ⓗ Ⓙ Ⓚ	15 Ⓐ Ⓑ Ⓒ Ⓓ Ⓔ	20 Ⓕ Ⓖ Ⓗ Ⓙ Ⓚ

TEST 3: Social Studies Reading

1 Ⓐ Ⓑ Ⓒ Ⓓ	7 Ⓐ Ⓑ Ⓒ Ⓓ	13 Ⓐ Ⓑ Ⓒ Ⓓ	19 Ⓐ Ⓑ Ⓒ Ⓓ
2 Ⓕ Ⓖ Ⓗ Ⓘ	8 Ⓕ Ⓖ Ⓗ Ⓘ	14 Ⓕ Ⓖ Ⓗ Ⓘ	20 Ⓕ Ⓖ Ⓗ Ⓘ
3 Ⓐ Ⓑ Ⓒ Ⓓ	9 Ⓐ Ⓑ Ⓒ Ⓓ	15 Ⓐ Ⓑ Ⓒ Ⓓ	21 Ⓐ Ⓑ Ⓒ Ⓓ
4 Ⓕ Ⓖ Ⓗ Ⓘ	10 Ⓕ Ⓖ Ⓗ Ⓘ	16 Ⓕ Ⓖ Ⓗ Ⓘ	22 Ⓕ Ⓖ Ⓗ Ⓘ
5 Ⓐ Ⓑ Ⓒ Ⓓ	11 Ⓐ Ⓑ Ⓒ Ⓓ	17 Ⓐ Ⓑ Ⓒ Ⓓ	23 Ⓐ Ⓑ Ⓒ Ⓓ
6 Ⓕ Ⓖ Ⓗ Ⓘ	12 Ⓕ Ⓖ Ⓗ Ⓘ	18 Ⓕ Ⓖ Ⓗ Ⓘ	24 Ⓕ Ⓖ Ⓗ Ⓘ

TEST 4: Natural Sciences Reading

1 Ⓐ Ⓑ Ⓒ Ⓓ	7 Ⓐ Ⓑ Ⓒ Ⓓ	13 Ⓐ Ⓑ Ⓒ Ⓓ	19 Ⓐ Ⓑ Ⓒ Ⓓ
2 Ⓕ Ⓖ Ⓗ Ⓘ	8 Ⓕ Ⓖ Ⓗ Ⓘ	14 Ⓕ Ⓖ Ⓗ Ⓘ	20 Ⓕ Ⓖ Ⓗ Ⓘ
3 Ⓐ Ⓑ Ⓒ Ⓓ	9 Ⓐ Ⓑ Ⓒ Ⓓ	15 Ⓐ Ⓑ Ⓒ Ⓓ	21 Ⓐ Ⓑ Ⓒ Ⓓ
4 Ⓕ Ⓖ Ⓗ Ⓘ	10 Ⓕ Ⓖ Ⓗ Ⓘ	16 Ⓕ Ⓖ Ⓗ Ⓘ	22 Ⓕ Ⓖ Ⓗ Ⓘ
5 Ⓐ Ⓑ Ⓒ Ⓓ	11 Ⓐ Ⓑ Ⓒ Ⓓ	17 Ⓐ Ⓑ Ⓒ Ⓓ	23 Ⓐ Ⓑ Ⓒ Ⓓ
6 Ⓕ Ⓖ Ⓗ Ⓘ	12 Ⓕ Ⓖ Ⓗ Ⓘ	18 Ⓕ Ⓖ Ⓗ Ⓘ	24 Ⓕ Ⓖ Ⓗ Ⓘ

Section Three:
Beyond the Tests

9. Follow Through:

MAKING THE MOST OF YOUR EFFORTS

What a relief! The test is over, you've turned in your paper, and you're free! Free—but not through. The whole point of a testing experience is not surviving it but making use of it.

Counselors or admissions officers, of course, will use your standardized test scores in making decisions about your life. Teachers will use your grades on exams and quizzes to determine your mark for the class. And you can make use of the experience, too. You can learn from your mistakes and from your successes, so that on the next test you'll do even better. Therefore, the best word to sum up the last step in any test-taking experience is: Review!

When you get your graded papers back, go over them by yourself and, if necessary, with your teacher. Figure out what the right answer was for any question you missed. If you still can't get it, ask. This is especially important for mistakes that surprise you, because unless you know what you're doing wrong, you won't be able to do it right. Skim through your correct answers and think about how you might have made them even better.

If you disagree with any of the marks, discuss them with your teacher, calmly and politely. A mistake may have been made in the scoring; and if not, it's important for you to understand exactly what happened. Also, you might not understand how the teacher did the grading. If the test was graded on a curve, for example, you might have gotten a 97% that was worth only a B if several others who took the test scored higher.

If you do feel that the test was graded unfairly, that too much weight was given to one question, or that one test counted for too much in the overall grade for a course (usually about one third of the grade is based on tests, with class participation and other projects counting two thirds), you would do well to discuss it with your guidance counselor or a school administrator.

UNRAVELING THOSE MYSTERIOUS NUMBERS

Scores on standardized tests are even more significant than grades on classroom exams. Your guidance counselor will often be able to give you a fairly clear picture of your strongest and weakest sections, so go over your scores carefully with him or her, or with another trained individual, again paying special attention to areas where your scores surprised you.

You will not automatically receive your test papers back, so if you think you would like to see how your scores were arrived at, find out the proper procedure before registering for the exam and follow it. If you find any errors in your papers, you have the right to challenge them: the test scorers are not always correct. Even if you find no mistakes, you benefit by any opportunity to look at your test, since it will help to improve your future scores.

STUDENT RIGHTS

In addition to protesting errors on standardized tests, as a student you have other rights as well. By law, you (or your parents—rules vary from state to state and according to the student's age) have the right to see all of your school records. If you wish them changed because you consider them inaccurate or unfair, you have a right to a school-system hearing on the matter.

Also, no one besides your school officials or your family is supposed to be able to see those records without authorization from you or your parents; and standardized tests include forms by which you give written permission before testing organizations can forward your scores to any schools to which you may be applying.

This is not to suggest that you do battle at every turn of your educational and test-taking career. But it is important that you receive fair treatment—otherwise, all the work you've put into studying and testing well will be wasted.

USING YOUR GRADES AS A GUIDE

You will also waste any testing experience if you do not use it as a stepping stone. One high-school boy who continually failed math and science tests simply let it depress him, until he came to believe that he was just too dumb for math and science. Another in the same situation asked for extra help and got permission to retake an important exam. One classroom test, no matter how well or poorly you do on it, can help you do better on the next one. If you do badly on a series of them, it's a signal for getting extra help so that you can turn yourself around.

Standardized tests are even more important guidance tools. Your teachers and counselors receive guidance packets along with virtually every standardized test your school gives. You, and in some cases your parents, would do well to go over the scores on important tests with a counselor, not just for interpretation of them but also for information about what they mean for your educational goals and needs.

For instance, a student who has not considered higher education but who scores exceptionally well on the tests might find help in getting scholarships that would make college possible. Or a counselor might recommend that a student who does poorly on the academically oriented tests take special aptitude tests to discover other talents.

Test takers who generally do well in school but can't seem to score high marks on the standardized exams would be advised to get extra help to prepare for the next batch.

Although you cannot retake the achievement and aptitude tests that your school requires, it is possible to take some privately sponsored exams, such as the SAT, more than once, although the procedure can be complicated. However tempting it may be to try to raise your score by retaking the test, it might not work out that way. So it's a good idea to seek advice before using this test-taking strategy.

Test success means more than getting the right answers; it means using a certain amount of strategy outside the testing room, too—and the same applies to the rest of your academic activities.

10. Making a Good Impression:

OTHER FACTORS IN SCHOOL SUCCESS

Tests, of course, are not all that school is about—and there's more to doing well academically than being reliable in classwork and doing your best on exams. Making a generally good impression in school can also make a difference in how well you do on tests, since teachers tend, both consciously and unconsciously, to give the benefit of the doubt when grading papers to those students whom they think well of.

That doesn't mean you have to be a "Richard" or a "Beth." Richard and Beth were the ones who were always buttering up my junior-high and high-school teachers and who always gloated over the flubs the rest of us made. A similar pair exists in every class. Who are they in yours?

WATCH YOUR IMAGE

Visualize the students in your class who do fairly well and give a good impression without making themselves obnoxious. Maybe you can pick up a few tips.

- They are probably fairly good looking. It's unfortunate but true: Studies have shown that teachers look more kindly on students who are attractive than on those who are less so. This doesn't mean you should go out and get a "nose job" or a new wardrobe on the basis of that information, but keep in mind that if you appear for class neatly groomed and dressed, you give the teacher the impression that you care about school.
- More importantly, they probably *do* appear for class, and appear *on time*. Since teachers work hard to prepare their instructional material, they naturally tend to resent students who miss part of it regularly or who interrupt it by late arrival.
- And they are usually *prepared* for class, or at least give the impression of being prepared. When teachers grade papers of students who seem to be consistent and reliable in their work, they are more likely to assume that the test will be a good one and that bad work is simply the result of a "bad day."
- They likely do their homework regularly and on time. If for some reason you aren't able to turn in an assignment, talk with the teacher about that *before* class begins.
- By not chatting or messing around in class, they convey a positive attitude. So save the horseplay for between classes or after school, and you'll save yourself a lot of grief.
- When they've missed a quiz or test, they go to the teacher and volunteer to make it up. When you've done badly or are having difficulty with the work, ask the teacher for help. This effort not only will help you directly by clear-

ing up trouble spots, but will also go a long way toward convincing a teacher that you are serious about the course. And as mentioned earlier, never simply walk out on a test with no effort, comment, or follow-up. That's not only self-defeating in itself, but it can be insulting to the teacher; remember that teachers are people, too, and they respond to the same kind of consideration as other people do.

• Your successful classmates probably manage to maintain a friendly but polite relationship with teachers without going overboard or making everyone else look bad.

Apple polishing isn't necessary, but anyone who's serious about doing well in school should give some thought to *image* polishing.

A QUICK WORD ABOUT CHEATING

You have probably heard since before you even started school that cheating is wrong: It is against the rules that people build society upon. And you've surely been told many times over that when you cheat by stealing someone else's work, you are only cheating yourself. Those points are certainly true, but you also undoubtedly know that cheating does go on in classrooms, and you've probably been witness to it yourself.

Mentally glance over the classroom once again. Visualize an exam, and you'll mostly likely "see" one girl revealing her paper to her neighbor, or a boy glancing at his hidden notes. Think about the time a teacher heaped praise on a project presented by a student who'd just been boasting about lifting the whole report straight from the encyclopedia or his older brother's term paper. How did you feel?

Making a Good Impression

If you are someone who works hard, that kind of cheating really hurts you, because it means that you aren't getting full credit for the work *you've* done. But what can you do about it? You understandably don't want to get a reputation as a snitch. Well, for just that reason, most schools have set up systems for the anonymous reporting of that kind of cheating. If you're not getting full value for your work because of the cheating going on around you, consider making use of this method.

And it goes without saying that you yourself should not consider cheating.

On a practical level, cheating always catches up with cheaters in one way or another. If they get in the habit of not doing their own work honestly, the time will come when there's no chance to cheat and they won't be able to produce the work. And from a more practical point of view, if cheaters get caught, all the hard work and image building in the world will never erase that fact from their record or that image from their teachers' minds. When they do well on a test, the question will always be: "Did they cheat?" When they do poorly on a test, they are much less likely to get the help or sympathy someone with an honest reputation would.

Besides that, if you follow the steps for studying and test taking outlined in this book, you yourself should never feel the need to cheat. You will know, for instance, well ahead of time that you're having a problem in a course, so that you can get help in advance. By so doing, you can make a good impression as well as solve your problem.

Many students who cheat do so because they think that preparing for exams is a mystery they'll never solve. Or they may feel under tremendous pressure to do well on tests because of a mistaken belief that good grades mark them as good people; bad ones as personal failures. You know that neither reason is true. As you've found out, the ability to test well simply means mastering the not-so-complicated skill of taking tests.

Just to assure yourself that you do now have the skill to study and take tests successfully, look over the final review of the procedures that follows.

11. Review!

Whether you are

- reading a chapter for homework,
- studying for an exam, or
- taking a test of any kind, the steps are the same:
    1. *Preview:* Find out what is required.
    2. *View:* Do what is required.
    3. *Review:* Check to see that you have done what is required.

Practice, Practice, Practice

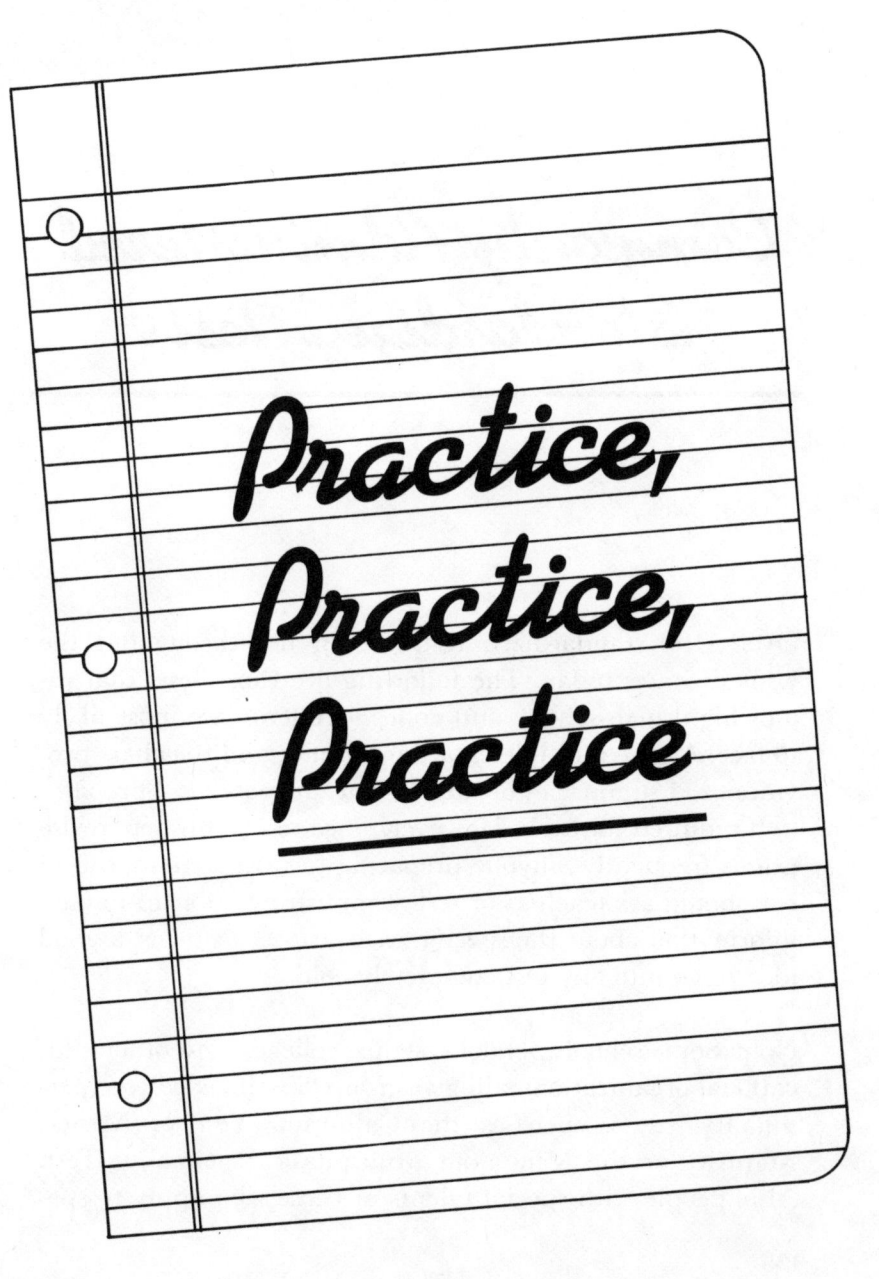

Commonly Administered Standardized Tests

Over 1100 standardized tests are in use throughout the United States today. The following are those tests that junior-high, high-school, and college students are most likely to face. All are multiple choice in format, and the chart provides brief summaries of the content, purpose, and preparation required for each. However, since test publishers revise exams frequently, anyone preparing to take a standardized test should ask teachers or test administrators for up-to-date information about the specific exam, since it's never a good idea to go into any test completely cold.

Note: Some schools, school systems, colleges, and other educational organizations still give group "intelligence" or "personality" tests, such as the California Test of Mental Maturity or the Minnesota Multiphasic Personality Test. Also, people with special talents or those who apply to specialized schools may take such specific standardized aptitude tests as the Seashore Tests of Musical Ability or the Bennett Mechanical Comprehension Test. Information on these types of tests is not included here because they are not widely administered. *However,*

- if you choose to have any of your special abilities tested, be aware that there is a test available for almost any skill or talent, and
- if you choose or are required to take a specialized test, find out as much about it beforehand as you can.

TEST	CONTENT
ACT (American College Testing Program)	English usage, math usage, social studies reading, science reading; "Interest Inventory" and "Student Profile" About 2 hours, 40 minutes
CAT (California Achievement Tests)	Reading: vocabulary and comprehension; grammar and punctuation; spelling; math computation and concepts; reference skills (research, maps, charts, etc.) About 2 hours, 50 minutes
CLEP (College Level Examination Program)	Exams in a wide variety of college-course subjects Time varies
CTBS (Comprehensive Tests of Basic Skills)	Reading, spelling, English usage, reference skills, science, social studies About 4 hours, 40 minutes
DAT (Differential Aptitude Test)	Eight tests designed to show skills in verbal, clerical, spatial, numerical, mechanical, logical, language, and spelling areas; "career planning" questionnaire

PURPOSE	PREPARATION
To measure skills related to college success; used by admissions offices to screen applicants; helps colleges guide and counsel students	Coaching is discouraged. Review grammar, math, social studies, and science for several months before test; work sample-test booklet
To measure achievement at all school grade levels in order to rate schools and to determine course assignments	Tests are designed to fit curricula, but review of past material is useful
To determine eligibility for college credit in courses not actually taken	Study materials on topics to be tested; review information booklet and samples
To measure knowledge gained and academic skills at all grade levels, in order to evaluate teaching quality and to place students appropriately	Content is geared to usual coursework, but review of past material is helpful
To provide information to students and administrators about best course of study, training, or career for student	No review needed or recommended; this is an exploration of talents rather than a test of knowledge

TEST	CONTENT
ERB (Educational Records Bureau) • CTP (Comprehensive Testing Program) • Achievement Tests • Admissions Tests	 Six tests in verbal and mathematical understanding and ability About 4½ hours Separate exams in English, foreign languages, and social studies Time varies ERB uses SSAT and its own math achievement test Time varies
GRE (Graduate Record Exam)	A general aptitude test like the SAT (*see below*), but on a more advanced level. Plus a separate aptitude test for the specific area in which one wishes to take postcollege education About 3 hours for the general section; times vary for the rest
ITED (Iowa Tests of Educational Development)	Seven tests in English expression, quantitative thinking, social studies, natural sciences, literature, vocabulary, and reference work About 4 hours

PURPOSE	PREPARATION
To provide information about students' achievement and potential ability in academic areas	Content is geared to coursework, but general review of past material is useful
To measure learning levels in various topics	Review past and present coursework in specific subject
To rate students applying to nonpublic secondary schools for screening purposes	Review past and recent work in English, science, math, and social studies
To screen applicants to graduate (postcollege) schools in specific academic subjects	Review college work in math, English, science, social science. Read carefully booklets sent, and work practice exams
To measure levels achieved in various academic areas, to provide schools and students with a profile of students' academic strengths and weaknesses	Though publisher advises not to study, review of material not currently in coursework won't hurt

TEST	CONTENT
Kuder General Interest Survey	Battery of items, each asking for personal preference from among three activities About 1 hour
Metro (Metropolitan Achievement Test)	Five tests in reading, math, language use, and (through 9th grade) science and social studies 2 to 4 hours
NEDT (National Educational Development Tests)	English usage, math usage, social studies reading, natural science reading, vocabulary
NMSQT (National Merit Scholarship Qualifying Test)	Same as the PSAT (see below) 1 hour, 40 minutes
OLMAT (Otis-Lennon Mental Abilities Test)	Verbal and nonverbal items designed to measure reasoning and comprehension abilities About 40 minutes
OLSAT (Otis-Lennon School Abilities Test)	Verbal, numerical, and shape items designed to predict performance in various academic areas About 45 minutes

PURPOSE	PREPARATION
To provide profile of individual's general interests, for guidance purposes	None
To measure knowledge and skills attained in various academic areas, both to rate education and to place students	Geared to coursework, but review of past and recent material is useful
To rate learning ability and achievement in grades 7–10, primarily for guidance purposes	None necessary, but a review of past work is useful
To screen applicants for eligibility to take exams to qualify for a number of scholarships available through the National Merit Scholarship Corporation	See PSAT, below. Students applying for scholarship exam must complete a special portion of information form given with the test
To measure problem-solving skills, primarily for guidance purposes	None
To measure academic aptitude, primarily for guidance purposes	None

TEST	CONTENT
OVIS (Ohio Vocational Interest Survey)	Over 250 job descriptions, each to be rated on a scale of preference; "career planner" chart About 45 minutes
PSAT (Preliminary Scholastic Aptitude Test)	About half verbal (vocabulary, usage, comprehension), and half math (concepts and computation) About 1 hour, 40 minutes
Regents (New York State Board of Regents Examinations)	Separate achievement tests for New York State high-school courses in the areas of business, English, foreign languages, math, science, and social studies Time varies
SAT (Scholastic Aptitude Test)	Verbal: antonyms, analogies, sentence completions, reading comprehension; mathematical: computation and "quantitative comparison" involving basic arithmetic, algebra, and geometry About 2½ hours

PURPOSE	PREPARATION
To provide a profile of an individual's career interests and talents, for guidance purposes	None
"Practice" for the SAT (see below): gives a preview of what to expect and where strengths and weaknesses are in academic talent. Offers advance guidance for school, college, or career planning	Review English and math; read student guide carefully; work sample test questions
To assess individuals' achievement in specific courses in order to grant graduation credit to students in schools under the jurisdiction of the New York Board of Regents (education supervisors)	Content of "Regents courses" is geared to exams; study material as for any final exam
To help screen applicants for college admission by measuring ability and potential for doing college work	Review English and math, using student guide as source of information for types of questions asked; practice sample tests

TEST	CONTENT
• TSWE (Test of Standard Written English)	Multiple-choice questions relating to English usage and grammar. Given with SAT About 30 minutes
SRA (Science Research Associates) • Achievement Tests	Reading, math, language arts, reference skills, social studies, science About 4 hours, 45 minutes
• Educational Ability Series	Verbal and nonverbal items designed to rate academic aptitude About 20 minutes
SSAT (Secondary School Admission Test)	Math: computation and problem-solving ability; verbal: synonyms and analogies; reading comprehension. (given in 2 levels of difficulty, depending on grade) About 1 hour, 15 minutes
Stanford Achievement Tests	Reading, vocabulary, spelling, language usage, math, science, social sciences About 3 to 5 hours, depending on grade level

PURPOSE	PREPARATION
To help colleges place students in proper courses. *Not* supposed to be used to screen applicants	Review grammar, punctuation, vocabulary, usage; practice sample tests
To measure academic achievement at all grade levels for guidance and placement purposes	Review past and current coursework; practice samples
Focuses on aptitude rather than achievement, for comparison and guidance	None
To screen applicants in grades 5 and up for admission to private or specialized junior and senior high schools	Review math and vocabulary; practice sample tests in student booklet
To measure achievement in various academic areas at all grade levels, for purposes of guidance and student placement	Review past and recent coursework

TEST	CONTENT
STEP Tests (Sequential Tests of Educational Progress)	Individual tests in reading, math, writing, listening, study skills, social science, science, reasoning
• SCAT (School and College Ability Test)	SCAT aptitude test often given with STEP tests. Each test is about 20–40 minutes long
ASVAB (Armed Forces Vocational Aptitude Battery)	Science, math, vocabulary, reading comprehension, aptitudes for coding, mechanical, and electrical skills. About 2 hours, 10 minutes
Minimum competency or "functional" tests	Basic reading and math needed for competent functioning in life, such as reading a want ad, making change. Content and format vary by school system

PURPOSE	PREPARATION
To measure academic knowledge and ability at all grade levels	Review coursework for appropriate test
	None
Used by Army and Navy to place recruits or enlistees in appropriate work. Portions used by Marine Corps and Air Force to screen applicants Given to junior and/or senior high school students to be sure they possess minimum skills before leaving school	Practice samples available from recruiting offices. Marine and Air Force applicants should review math and English Those weak in basic skills should review

Sources for Further Information

Since a single book may not be able to fully cover each individual's strengths and weaknesses, here are some other resources that can help you to practice the particular study and test-taking skills you need.

BOOKS AND STUDY GUIDES

The books listed below are among the better guides to studying and test taking. Any that are not in local bookstores can probably be found in school or public libraries or on the shelves in guidance counselors' offices. They can also be ordered directly from the publisher. Most are for the college-level and above reader, but they lay out the facts and tips clearly and simply.

Bracy, Jane and Marian McClintock. *Read to Succeed.* New York: McGraw-Hill, 1975.

An excellent guide to studying and test taking as well as effective reading.

Colligan, Louise, and Doug Colligan. *The A Plus Guide to Good Grades.* New York: Scholastic Book Services, 1979.

Tips from a teacher on overall school success, with a good section on writing papers.

Divine, Dr. James H., and David W. Kylen. *How to Beat Test Anxiety and Score Higher on the SAT and All Other Exams.* Woodbury, N.Y.: Barron's Educational Series, 1982.

Despite its overblown title, this is a very good book full of sound advice on coping with exams and with the fear of them.

Feder, Bernard. *The Complete Guide to Taking Tests.* Englewood Cliffs, N.J.: Prentice-Hall, 1979.

A fine book full of facts about testing and tips on how to approach all exams. (Out of print—check the library.)

Kalina, Sigmund. *How to Sharpen Your Study Skills.* New York: Lothrop, Lee & Shepard, 1975.

Basic tips for younger readers. A good summary.

Langan, John. *Reading and Study Skills.* New York: McGraw-Hill, 1978.

Written with the college student in mind, but with useful advice for anyone.

Lorayne, Harry. *Good Memory—Good Student.* Briarcliff Manor, N.Y.: Stein & Day, 1976 (paperback).

> Tips on effective remembering from a man who based his career on making his memory work.

Lyman, Howard B. *Test Scores and What They Mean,* 3d ed. Englewood Cliffs, N.J.: Prentice-Hall, 1978.

> An explanation of the sense and significance of "all those numbers," written for adults.

Smith, Donald E. P., ed. *Learning to Learn.* New York: Harcourt, Brace and World, 1961.

> A good, step-by-step technique for studying and test taking.

Wikler, Janet. *How to Study and Learn.* New York: Franklin Watts, 1978.

> Careful advice, written for younger readers.

TEST-TAKING WORKBOOKS

Paperback guides on the order of "How to Score a Zillion on the XYZ Exam" cram the shelves of many bookstores. The problem lies not in finding one or several for a specific exam but in finding one that is worth the money and the effort. Some guidelines for choosing:

• Beware any that promise absolute success or instant results.

• Avoid any that rely on "secret systems" like playing hunches or "going for the middle answer."

Sources for Further Information

- Check the copyright dates! Any that offer tips for a specific test but that are more than a year or two old are likely to be too far out of date to be useful. The better series update their workbooks annually or as the tests change.
- Look for thick sections of sample exams, since practicing is vital.

Here are the names and addresses of publishers that produce the better workbook series, with individual guides to almost every test:

Arco Publishing Co., Inc., 219 Park Avenue South, New York, New York 10003

Barron's Educational Series, Inc., 113 Crossways Park Drive, Woodbury, New York 11797

Fireside, Simon & Schuster, Inc., 1230 Avenue of the Americas, New York, New York 10020

HBJ Test Preparation Series, Harcourt, Brace, and Jovanovich, Inc., 1250 Sixth Avenue, San Diego, California 92101

LANGUAGE SKILLS STUDY GUIDES

One of the best ways to prepare for *any* standardized test is to strengthen overall language skills. These are some useful self-trainers:

Bromberg, Murray, Lulius Liebb, Arthur Traiger. *Barron's 504 Absolutely Essential Words*. Woodbury, N.Y.: Barron's, 1975.

Brown, James I. *Reading Power.* Lexington, Mass.: D.C. Heath, 1978.

Lewis, Norman. *Correct Spelling Made Easy.* New York: Dell, 1963.

———. *Word Power Made Easy.* New York: Pocket Books, 1978.

TEST PUBLISHERS

The following are the major publishers or developers of the most commonly administered standardized tests. Guidance counselors and test administrators receive packets of information and samples (which they should share with test takers) from them before a test is given, and many publishers distribute such packets directly to test takers and their families. Anyone who wishes information about a specific test or about a type of test may also request it directly by writing to the publisher's Public Information Office or Marketing Department with the request and the reason for it. Some samples and descriptions are free, and some require a small fee.

Addison-Wesley Testing Service
South Street
Reading, Massachusetts 01867

Produces and distributes Educational Testing Service tests and others.

Sources for Further Information

American College Testing Program
P.O. Box 168
Iowa City, Iowa 52243

> ACT entrance exams and guidance materials.

College Entrance Examination Board
888 Seventh Avenue
New York, New York 10106

> An organization of 2500 educational institutions and systems that sponsors a wide variety of tests and distributes information on the SAT, CLEP, PSAT, and other standardized exams, as well as guidance materials.

CTB/McGraw-Hill
DelMonte Research Park
Monterey, California 93940

> CAT, CTBS, and other tests.

Educational Records Bureau
Box 619
Princeton, New Jersey 08541

> An organization of private and public schools and colleges that manages the CTP exams.

Educational Testing Service
Princeton, New Jersey 08541

> CTP, STEP, PSAT, SAT, SSAT, CLEP, GRE, and other tests and educational programs.

The Psychological Corporation
Harcourt, Brace, and Jovanovich
757 Third Avenue
New York, New York 10017

   Stanford, Metro, Otis-Lennon, DAT, OVIS, and many specialized personality, aptitude, talent, and ability tests.

Science Research Associates, Inc.
155 N. Wacker Drive
Chicago, Illinois 60606

   SRA Achievement, Iowa Tests, Kuder, and some other more specialized exams.

ORGANIZATIONS

These groups and agencies can provide help and information about various aspects of studying and testing. School counselors and libraries are also good sources for guides and other help for test-taking and study skills.

American School Counselors Association
American Personnel and Guidance Association
5203 Leesburg Pike
Falls Church, Virginia 22046

   Has information about testing organizations and procedures.

National Association of Secondary School Principals
1904 Association Drive
Reston, Virginia 22091

Has produced an excellent workbook entitled "Improving College Admission Scores" and, with the American Council on Education, a most useful series of study skills workbooks.

National Education Association
1201 16th Street, NW
Washington, DC 20036

Can provide direction to a variety of sources for guidance and help through its Information Office.

National Institute of Education
U.S. Department of Education
400 Maryland Avenue, SW
Washington, DC 20024

Has available pamphlets and information about testing and other educational concerns.

COACHING AND TUTORING SCHOOLS

Anyone who feels the need of a tutor or a "cram school" for help with coursework or for prepping for standardized tests should choose carefully. Since there are no lists of "approved" or "effective" coaching operations, students and their families must screen these services for themselves. Here are some tips and guidelines:

• Ask for recommendations from teachers, guidance counselors, other families, and students. Local colleges or universities may have tutors available for specific subjects.
• When you have a list of names, ask the Better Business

Bureau and your local consumer agency about any complaints that might be recorded against the coaching businesses on the list. Ask those who have used the more informal tutors about their styles and effectiveness.

- From that narrowed-down list, be sure to inquire about fees and schedules, *and* about "success rates": how many of their students have raised grades in school, or what are their average scores on important standardized tests? Ask for names to contact.
- Just as important as cost and reliability is compatibility: If you don't like the tutor or the coach, you're not going to learn much, so when you've focused on the "best" ones, pick someone you seem to get along with.
- *Beware* any individual or organization (or book) that "guarantees" improved performance in school or improved scores on standardized tests, especially if that "guarantee" comes at high cost! Your own good efforts offer your only guarantee.

Index

A
ACT (American College Testing Program), 7, 114, 118, 119, 122, 123, 140
ASVAB (Armed Forces Vocational Aptitude Battery), 150

B
Bennett Mechanical Comprehension Test, 139

C
California Test of Mental Maturity, 138
CAT (California Achievement Tests), 140
cheating, 132-134
classwork, 34

CLEP (College Level Examination Program), 140
cramming, 12, 39, 52, 107
CTBS (Comprehensive Tests of Basic Skills), 140
CTP (Comprehensive Testing Program), 142
curve, 79

D
DAT (Differential Aptitude Test), 117, 140
desensitization, 47-49

E
Europe, 97
extra credit, 78-79

F
finals, 80-94

G
goals, 31, 41
grades, 6, 55, 58, 77-79, 102-105, 126-128
GRE (Graduate Record Exam), 142

H
homework, 40, 131

I
instructions, 15-24, 114-115
ITED (Iowa Tests of Educational Development), 7, 142

K
Kuder General Interest Survey, 144

L
languages, 86
learning, latent, 13
learning, styles of, 32-33, 89

M
math, 86
memorizing, 39, 87-91
memory, 87
memory aids, 89-91
Metro (Metropolitan Achievement Test), 144
midterms, 80-94
Minnesota Multiphasic Personality Test, 138
motivation, 33, 46-47, 131

N
NEDT (National Educational Development Tests), 7, 144
New York State Board of Regents Examinations, 146
NMSQT (National Merit Scholarship Qualifying Test), 144
note taking, 34-35, 37

O
OLMAT (Otis-Lennon Mental Abilities Test), 144
OLSAT (Otis-Lennon School Abilities Test), 144
OVIS (Ohio Vocational Interest Survey), 146

P
percentile, 104
perfectionism, 31-32
procrastinating, 31
proctor, 112-113
PSAT (Preliminary Scholastic Aptitude Test), 108, 112, 146
psychology, educational, 4, 97

Q
quartile, 104
questions, kinds of
essay, 11, 25, 68-77, 85, 102

Index

multiple choice, 8-9, 11, 25, 64-66, 102, 115
problem solving, 8, 11, 66-67, 86, 107-108
short answers, 11, 25, 59-64, 85-86, 102
true-false, 7, 8, 10, 63-64, 102
quizzes, 54-58

R
relaxation, 25, 52, 91
relaxation techniques, 39, 49-51
rights, student, 128

S
SAT (Scholastic Aptitude Test), 7, 9, 108, 112, 114, 129
SCAT (School and College Ability Test), 150
science, 86
Seashore Tests of Musical Ability, 139
skimming, 36-37, 38
SRA (Science Research Associates), 7, 120, 121, 148
SSAT (Secondary School Admission Test), 7, 112, 148
Stanford Achievement Tests, 148
stanine, 104
statistics, 113
STEP (Sequential Tests of Educational Progress), 150
studying, 29-30

T
test anxiety, 42-46
test site, 113
tests
  achievement, 99-100, 109
  aptitude, 99, 100, 109
  guessing on, 7, 9, 23, 64
  importance of, 1, 5-6, 10, 55
  intelligence, 99, 100-101
  minimum competency, 6, 100, 150
  personality, 99, 101
  retaking, 129
  standardized, 6, 7, 9, 95-123
  take-home, 86-87
time, organization of, 39-41, 69
TSWE (Test of Standard Written English), 148

U
U.S. Army, 97

V
vocabulary, 108

W
walking out, 92-94, 132
World War I, 97